SUE JOHNSON

THE ALTERNATE ENCYCLOPEDIA

Tweed Museum of Art, University of Minnesota Duluth

Sue Johnson: The Alternate Encyclopedia

This catalogue is published in an edition of 3000 on the occasion of an exhibition at the Tweed Museum of Art, University of Minnesota Duluth,
January 27 – March 28, 2004.

Catalogue design by Stephanie L. Magedanz

ISBN 1-889523-28-3

Tweed Museum of Art
University of Minnesota Duluth
1201 Ordean Court
Duluth, MN 55812
(218) 726-8222
fax (218) 726-8503
tma@d.umn.edu
www.tweedmuseum.org

This project is funded in part by the Minnesota State Arts Board by an appropriation from the Minnesota Legislature and the National Endowment for the Arts; the Alice Tweed Tuohy Foundation; and UMD Student Service Fees.

This activity is made possible in part by a grant from the Minnesota State Arts Board, through an appropriation by the Minnesota State Legislature and a grant from the National Endowment for the Arts.

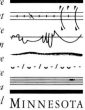

MINNESOTA STATE ARTS BOARD

Front Cover:
Free Association Spelling Book, 2002-2003
unique prints, relief and Xerox-transfer with pencil, 17 x 18"

Vintage school desk-chair, ca 1950's
Wood, metal 31 x 33 x 24"

Back Cover:
New Ark Preservation Project, 2002-2003
found objects encased in plastic Foodsaver™ bags,
average size 1 x 10 x 11", vintage table and chairs

Table of Contents

ALTERNATE TABLE OF CONTENTS

Prairie dog hears big secret - Spelling bees suspended across the globe - Hair transformed - Whale with no tail cries alligator tears - Paul Bunyan visits the Pyramids - Lady scientist revolutionizes how we see the world - New species of naval orange discovered with smile on its face - Evidence misleads noted historian - Tasty luncheon dishes prepared with weird fish - Myth of Pegasus revealed - Snakes in liquid - The last buffalo sighted in Duluth - Common workman's wrench and deep-sea shrimp are relatives - Microscope uncovers hidden matriarchal world - Plastic bags prove their worth - Women drivers do not cause more accidents - Clash of the Giant Duck and the Over-grown Sparrow - Photographic proof of oddities - Olive loaf aids digestion - The bird-woman is real – Scientific evidence confirms prince used to be a frog - Squirrels say 'cheese' for the camera – Panty hose linked to snake ritual – Many books damaged when hot chocolate spilled in library – Startling proof offered that moon is made of compressed moon-rock material – Local zoo now empty.

ACKNOWLEDGEMENTS

i

First and foremost, our thanks go to artist Sue Johnson for her technically adept, thought-provoking, and often humorous work, for her superior organizational skills, and for her full participation in all phases of this project. Camille Norton wrote a series of five poems specifically for the exhibition and publication, and she deserves our thanks for so succinctly ensnaring Johnson's visuals with words. Stephanie Magedanz is responsible for the beautifully effective design of this catalogue, for which Steve Bardolph produced a series of wonderful installation photographs. A rather complicated exhibition design was rendered legible and navigable by preparator Peter Weizenegger, assisted by Will Bartsch. Along with the artist's own collections, objects in the exhibition were lent by the: Minnesota Historical Society, St. Paul; St. Louis County Historical Society, Duluth; UMD Department of Biology, and by Rose LaGrosse, Molly B. Larson and Sandi Peterson. For its exhibitions and publications, the Tweed Museum of Art is grateful for support from: the Alice Tweed Tuohy Foundation; the Minnesota State Arts Board by an appropriation through the Minnesota State Legislature and a grant from the National Endowment for the Arts; Tweed Museum Members; and the University of Minnesota Duluth School of Fine Arts and Student Services Fees.

The artist expresses her thanks to the following individuals and institutions:

Colby Caldwell
Mark Gulezian
Jean Illingworth
James Mowry
Camille Norton
Robert Paul
John Pastor
Andrea Pollan
Peter Spooner
Christopher Tanner
Minnesota Historical Society
St. Louis County Historical Society
The Virginia Center for the Creative Arts
American Antiquarian Society
Art Omi International Artist Colony
Pollock-Krasner Foundation
St. Mary's College of Maryland Foundation
The MacDowell Colony
Ragdale Foundation

Works in this exhibition were produced with the assistance of Art Omi International Artist Colony, the American Antiquarian Society, St. Mary's College of Maryland Foundation, The MacDowell Colony, Pyramid Atlantic, The Ragdale Foundation, and The Virginia Center for the Creative Arts.

Opposite page:
Self–Portrait as an artist-naturalist, Loplop's Sister (after Max Ernst) oil on linen, 2000–01, 38 x 50"
Collection of Tweed Museum of Art, Sax Purchase Fund

Object: The Last Buffalo (red velvet chair with buffalo horns), n.d. (ca. early 20th c.)
buffalo horns, fabric over wood, 36 x 28 x 27"
Collection of St. Louis County Historical Society.

Object: Prairie Chicken (Tympanuchus cupido)
taxidermied bird specimen, 16 x 14 x 16 1/2"
Collection of the Department of Biology,
University of Minnesota Duluth.

Sue Johnson

The Alternate Encyclopedia

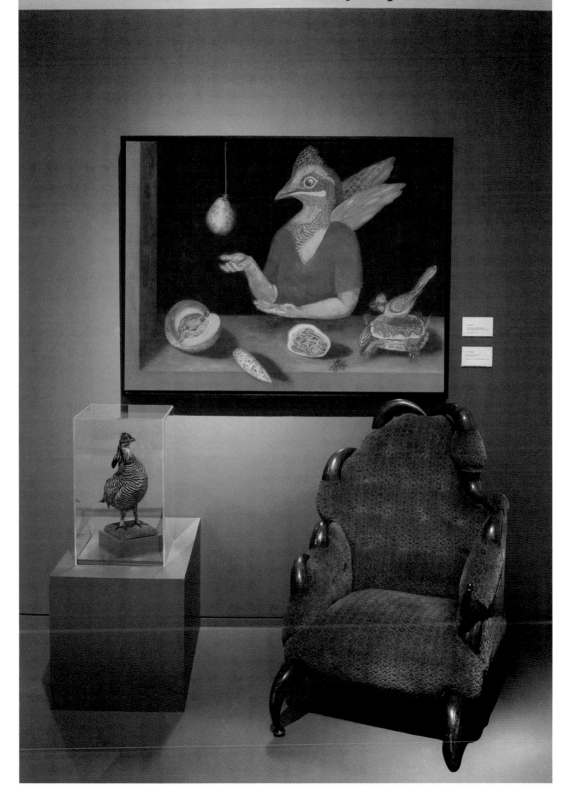

(THE ARTIST AS)
SURREALVISIONARYMORPHICNATURALIST

On the left, one stuffed prairie chicken. On the right, one overstuffed chair with buffalo horn arms and legs. On the wall between and behind, Sue Johnson's painting *Self portrait as an artist-naturalist (Loplop's sister)*. Besides eliciting a palpable sense of the surreal (which orbits around all of her work), this tableaux serves as a fitting introduction to the many strategies and concerns of Johnson's current work:

1) nature stilled and dissected for analysis, study and pictorial representation;
2) nature transformed into objects of culture;
3) homage to and critique of the history of nature's representation by art and science;
4) the evidence of these transactions renamed, displayed, and catalogued;
5) the evidence disseminated.
6) Begin a new chapter.

Trained as a painter and printmaker, Johnson found herself thinking about natural history engravings while working on a series of large paintings of microscopic specimens. Too big to be believable, she scaled them down and turned to printmaking and watercolor, the historically preferred medium of artist-naturalists. Perhaps not completely realizing the effect it would have on her future work, it was at that point that she adopted the form of the encyclopedia. Strategizing about how to display some of these first prints, Johnson collected objects to install with them. Voila! (Eureka!) *The Alternate Encyclopedia was born.*

A decade-old project, *The Alternate Encyclopedia* is structured like a hall of natural history, with a rotating series of themed 'cabinets of curiosity', at once divided and linked by themes or 'chapters' that Johnson imposes on them. The very titles she chooses for these themes mimic, and are sometimes lifted from, headings found in encyclopedias written for popular audiences, marking her preference for information that is a bit (or more) out of date, and at times, a bit (or more) off the wall. Cultivating Young Minds. The New Wonder World. Scientific American Woman. Wild Animals I Have Known. Travel and Exploration. So ingrained into Johnson's practice are the five themed chapters that comprise this version of *The Alternate Encyclopedia* that close scrutiny of any one soon reveals traces of the other four. *Travel and Exploration*, for example, first announces its concern with post-war leisure time travel and car culture, but when outlined in more detail, is seen to contain subtexts of:

1) Scientific American Women
   A. Gender, feminist practice, historically "acceptable" roles for women in science
      1. souvenir lady's shoe with waterfall on its ceramic toe
      2. Mountie Barbie
      3. Mom becomes mobile
   B., C., etc… (keep looking, there is always more)

2) Wild Animals I Have Known
  A. Relationships between human and
     animals, man-made objects with animal
     characteristics
     1. Paul Bunyan and Babe
     2. Association of regions with their
        stereotypical animal ambassadors
3) New Wonder World
  A. Genetic engineering, morphing, mutation,
     merging of nature/culture
     1. The automobile/beast/mythic figure -
        Mustang, Cougar, Mercury
     2. Retooling the landscape for the
        automobile
     3. Taming nature for human comfort
4. Cultivating Young Minds
  A. Travel as education, travel to natural and
     historic monuments, travel with
     Mom and Dad
     1. The cultured nature of the world as
        museum
     2. Education from the car-seat, travel
        magazines, road signage, brochures
     3. Homes away from home

As art, *The Alternate Encyclopedia* is by turns quite
simple and incredibly complex. Simple, because its
step-by-step procedures are easy to follow: collect,
name, illustrate, display, store. Complex, because
these seemingly simple procedures give rise to
exponentially increasing possibilities for extra-
aesthetic connections. At the same time, it is
Johnson's aesthetic, a blend of believable
illustration, thoughtfully chosen subject (and
object), together with a curatorial panache, that
makes it all work. Wherever *The Alternate
Encyclopedia* is shown, local collections can be
mined for their temporary contributions to the
project. Like many contemporary artists, Johnson
has made the museum, its collections and
practices of display and interpretation and
important part of her overall project.

The root word "morph," with uses related to both
language and to organic forms, had its origin as
"shape" in the original Greek. In our current
global-culture, internet-connected Post-modern
soup of a world, it has redefined itself to describe
virtual transformations from one digitally
visualized thing to another, a transformation that
is computer-driven, determined by and coded as
mathematical information. Although she does use
new technologies to produce some of her work,
Sue Johnson does her morphing the old
fashioned way.

morphosis n. [G. *morphosis*, proces of forming
< morphoun, to form.] 1. The manner in which an organism
or one of its parts changess form or the manner or order of its
development.

morphology n. [G. *morphologie*, coined (1822) by J. W. von
Goethe < Gr. morphe form + -logie, LOGY] 1. The branch
of biology that deals with the form and structure of animals
and plants 2. A) the branch of linguistics that deals with the
internal structure and forms of words: with syntax, it forms a
division of grammar b) the study of the structure,
classification, and relationships of morphemes 3. Any scientific
study of form and structure, as in physical geography 4. Form
and structure, as of an organism, regarded as a whole. -
Websters New World Dictionary, Second College Edition

−Peter F. Spooner, Curator

Interview

Compiled from conversations between Sue Johnson and Peter Spooner on two occasions; October 25, 2003 in New York City, and by phone December 7, 2003.

PS Let's begin by talking about how the exhibition is organized.

SJ The entire exhibition space is designed to be a quasi "Alice in Wonderland" encyclopedia, where information is very big and we are very small, with viewers traveling through five themed chapter-worlds. *Cultivating Young Minds* is focused on the young reader and how early encounters with pictures, both popular and scientific, frame one's view of the world. The *Wild Animals I Have Known* chapter, named after an 1899 book by the same name that sought to tell "true nature stories" for a popular audience, focuses on tamed and wild nature and the deconstruction of mythological creatures. The goal of *Travel and Exploration* is to juxtapose 19th century exploration of America against the popularized tourism of the 20th century made possible by, among other inventions and conveniences, the automobile. Mother Nature, the historical exclusion of women from the ranks of scientists, the 19th century identification of horticulture and botany as approved feminine pursuits, and the shifting roles of women are at the heart of *Scientific American Woman*. Work in *The New Wonder World* explores contemporary issues such as genetic engineering and species extinction and mutation.

PS Traditional encyclopedias might organize information under such headings.

SJ Unlike the more typical A-Z organization, the exhibition installation is actually a take off on a style of organizing encyclopedias in the late 19th and early 20th century that grouped information into thematic areas. Many times these were one-volume encyclopedias, which presented compendiums of practical everyday information like *Collier's Cyclopedia of Social and Commercial Information and Treasury of Useful and Entertaining Knowledge*. Included among the seventy-seven thematic headings are Hints to Stammerers, Brief History of the United States, The Cultivation of Fruits, Drowning, Home Studies for Young Ladies, Phrenology, and Agriculture and Physics without Appliances. *The Book of Popular Science*, a series published by the Grolier Society in the 1920s featured different entries from volume to volume under fixed chapter headings: The Universe, The Earth, Life, Plant Life, Animal Life, Man, Health, Power, Commerce, Industry, Society, Biography, and Household Science. And *Compton's Pictured Encyclopedia* in the 1920s and 30s devised a slightly different strategy of fixed headings; Tales for the Story Hour, School and Home, Highlights in History's Pageant, The Story of Presidents, Some Famous Men and Women, Travel-views at Home and Abroad, The World of Work and Play, Guideposts to Literature, Art and Music, Rambles through Factland, and Wonders We Call Life. Departing from traditional A-Z taxonomies, these publishers embraced a more poetic response to the organization of information, one that hints at the impossibility of content coverage under the growing weight of "facts" in the 20th century. From our vantage point today, these systems might seem somewhat odd in the way they juxtapose, for example, everyday practical advice and hard science, or for example, the story of Galileo's life and the choice of a hobby.

PS We could say that that this method of organizing information in printed form was influenced by the "cabinet of curiosities" collections of the 17th and 18th centuries. With diverse objects belonging to one collector coming from many different places and reflecting many different bodies of knowledge - artworks, natural history specimens - all in one place.

SJ Certainly there are parallels with cabinets of curiosities, which were so popular in The Netherlands, Germany, Italy, France, England and beyond. Emperor Rudolph II of Prague, Peter the Great and the Medici were responsible for assembling vast collections. Well-to-do but ordinary citizens of The Netherlands were able to amass small and large collections of exotic items collected on the trade routes of the Dutch East India Company and other New World expeditions. Collectors like Fredeick Ruysch and Peter the Great assembled comprehensive yet eclectic collections of oddities found in nature, including human specimens. Exotic flora and fauna, oddities, rarities, gold encrusted objects fashioned with natural materials - all these and more found their way into the collector's cabinet. Some collections were unabashedly idiosyncratic owing to an individual collector's aesthetic choices. Conversely, some attempted to devise a new system for organizing the natural world. Sometimes the system made taxonomic sense, sometimes a more intuitive aesthetic was at work.

PS But they were organized nonetheless.

SJ Absolutely. My categories attempt to emulate a particular type of encyclopedia, aimed at a popular everyday audience. There is sense of trying to organize materials into groups of basic information that everyone should know and that presents information in a way that provides a sense of wonder. Among many sources of inspiration I am quite fond of Jorge Luis Borges' literary navigations through systems of order and knowledge, and in particular his fiction that renders a "certain Chinese encyclopedia, the celestial Emporium of Benevolent Knowledge" that divides animals into the following categories: "a) belonging to the Emperor, b) embalmed, c) tame, d) sucking pigs, e) sirens, f) fabulous, g) stray dogs, h) included in the present classification, i) frenzied, j) innumerable, k) drawn with a very fine camelhair brush, l) et cetera, m) having just broken the water pitcher, n) that from a long way off look like flies."

PS So what is Sue Johnson's method of organizing information?

SJ It seems to me that systems of knowledge that attempt to organize the dynamics of life into one fixed system must be at some level inconsistent, incomplete, unfinished, and in the end, quite idiosyncratic. This is of real interest to me. And so when I was developing the thematic setting for this particular show, with its categories of *Cultivating Young Minds, Travel and Exploration*, and so on, it was not meant to be holistic but instead to call attention to the system itself.

PS It's fragmented.

SJ Yes, and in fact the last exhibition I had was actually called "Fragments from the Alternate Encyclopedia," because of the sense that an encyclopedia cannot cover everything, or that it can be a subjective enterprise, influenced by the subjectivity of the person organizing it.

PS The way the categories are chosen may be rather fleeting, due to subjective interests, as opposed to universal and lasting.

SJ And certainly the things that are under each category are in no way meant to be comprehensive either.

PS Is this because of the fact that a true encyclopedia is an impossibility? There is so much we don't know, and so much we can't or haven't yet synthesized with prior knowledge. We are constantly learning new things, and trying to incorporate them into what we do know - so an encyclopedia is at best a vain attempt at cataloguing everything we think we know at a certain point.

SJ The struggle I think we have in the 20th century, and actually going back to the 16th century is the assumption that an encyclopedia can actually offer this comprehensive view. What you find historically is that there's a breakdown in the idea of encyclopedic knowledge. One thing that happens in the 20th century is that encyclopedias begin to have updates. You'd get updates in the mail and you were meant to put them in a three-ring binder or add them to your shelf. But there was no was to go back and delete the information that was invalid, the things that were no longer true or were superseded by new information. With the updates, there was a belief that with more information you could somehow still provide this comprehensive body of knowledge. I think this is something we still believe – we still have encyclopedias. With encyclopedias on the Web, we've created a situation where information actually can be deleted and replaced with updates. Anything that exists in hard copy, is potentially problematic which ultimately is what my project is about – the visual image that survives. It's about what happens when ideas get drawn or painted or written in text, that is then treated as an historical artifact. Nothing really gets updated, and therefore retains its veracity. That becomes the

basis for my work, and how I think about it.

PS So the *Alternate Encyclopedia* is grounded in earlier thinking about atlases and encyclopedias, that if a thing was written, drawn, and published, it somehow had to be true. They are assumed to be authoritative, and there is no way to change them. In the same sense, you can't change a work of art once it's set down. It stands for the moment it was created.

SJ It is fixed.

PS It's fixed, visually and physically. Now with computers and the internet, the ability exists to update, edit and link knowledge and levels of knowledge - to bring in ideas, images, and opinions from many places onto one surface or area, into one time frame, and to have individual users sampling or mixing their own "knowledge salads."

SJ I love that notion of "knowledge salads – it's both domestic and about consumption. Of course we are operating in a system of parallel realities, because while we've got the Web that does all of these things, we also live in a world that has museums, and natural history exhibits that remain fixed, and there is little attempt to reconcile these different ways that we process and collect information. My sense is that today's youth who have grown up on the World Wide Web have the sense that information is constantly updated and that it's the "right" information. They seem perfectly content to bring together ideas, images and opinions from many places into one time frame, and to have individual users sampling or mixing their own "knowledge salads". From teaching, I'm very aware that my students will not go to the library first, they'll go to the internet. Because it's this place of "truth."

PS It's the new truth.

SJ Yes. But at the same time everything else we're doing in culture is very much about fixed notions. We still have an institutional structure that is not as fluid as this new technology. On the other hand, maybe that's my perspective as a member of an older generation, a generation that knew the the "olden days" before the Web. Maybe it is all fluid. "Random," as my students would say. My experience though is that we live in a world where there are at least two types of systems; the fixed and the fluid. So in practical terms we have these experiences that constantly have to be mediated as we remind ourselves that this is just one person's opinion, that "x" is subjective, that this museum display was designed and wall labels written by a human being with a particular point of view, as opposed to the way we think about the Web as being more objective, but of course it's not. It's this contemporary condition that I'm very interested in, and I'm using the guise of an older system juxtaposed to how we operate today.

PS Do you think that we really want to rely on that older system? That an older generation may want its information to be a bit more solid and fixed? Or at least to have that appearance, as opposed to something that's constantly shifting.

SJ Right. I think the idea that there is no fixed truth is scary to us. That's the whole Postmodern dilemma.

PS Exactly. The whole concept of the Internet, with information constantly flowing in and flowing out is a very Postmodern notion. That nothing is ever the single, authoritative truth, that everything has some validity at some level, and can influence and color those things we once assumed to be fixed, or true.

SJ Ultimately it is very exhausting. If everything is in flux and nothing is fixed, there is this desire to want to hold onto even a momentary truth.

PS Anything…

SJ Yes, and so these individual, idiosyncratic systems become very intriguing and attractive, I think, in a contemporary environment.

PS This is why we have an ongoing argument about painting. Painting is dead! No it's not! Yes it is! Well, it was dead, but look, it's been resurrected! That's why painting is never really dead, because we do need, at least momentarily, to rely on or touch base with some fixed notion, whether in the form of a painting, a literary text, or some core of ideas we can hold on to.

SJ And a painting is also about the individual – about individual experience. Which runs counter to some of the ways we experience other pieces of visual information, like in the media. In this installation of *The Alternate Encyclopedia*, I intend for the individual chapters to both contain and signal a shifting of voice, thereby focusing attention on issues of authorship, exposing a sense of the individual who constructed the information. To heighten this sense, printmaking is used to mimic and comment on how information is actually disseminated on a large scale. Printing techniques change as if in response to new technologies or market conditions that would allow either expensive color or more economical black and white printing, or photographic reproduction. Some are unique watercolor paintings, offering the idea that artwork might have been commissioned by a wealthy patron, or might have served as the camera-ready artwork for a mass-produced publication. There are also stylistic shifts. All this, I hope, draws attention to the issue of authorship and the individual as collector and organizer of information.

PS Can you talk a little about the objects you collect?

SJ In *Re-producing Nature*, the items – the little souvenir Florida orange cup with the face on it, or the tortoise shell carving, or the 1950's

continued on page 16

CULTIVATING YOUNG MINDS

Early Genetic Engineering for Kids
Creepy Crawlers® toy, circa 1960's;
specimen display box with plastic insects.

From the outset, the chapter heading "cultivating young minds" announces Johnson's work as serious and authoritative, but at the same time suspect, since we have all grown up to revise part (if not most) of the formal education we received as children. A primary purpose of the illustrations and texts of encyclopedias is the dissemination of knowledge. Accordingly, Johnson often uses educational materials, objects and stories from her own childhood as a foil for her current work, at the same time admitting an attraction to information once authoritative but now out-of-date. *Free-Association Spelling Book* is both an evocation of early classroom learning and a gender-specific commentary, demonstrating how

the "chapters" of Johnson's overall project often overlap. The *Abstractions* (overpainted classroom anatomy charts) take familiar forms and alter their meaning by adding new information. *Early Genetic Engineering for Kids* demonstrates how a toy/instrument that allowed Johnson and her childhood peers to "make their own insects" presaged the current realities of genetic engineering. Watercolor "specimen pages" of animal characters from children's stories swap their literary form for a visual one, emphasizing aspects of the stories that exist as subtexts, like the lusty, pseudo-sexual undercurrents of *The Frog Prince*.

Free Association Spelling Book, 2002–2003
Unique prints, relief and
Xerox-transfer with pencil, 17 x 18"

Compact, 2002–2003

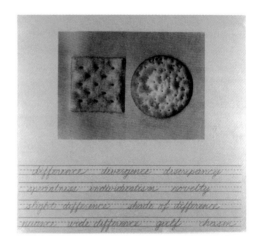

Difference, 2002-2003

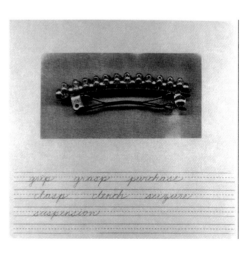

Grip, 2002-2003

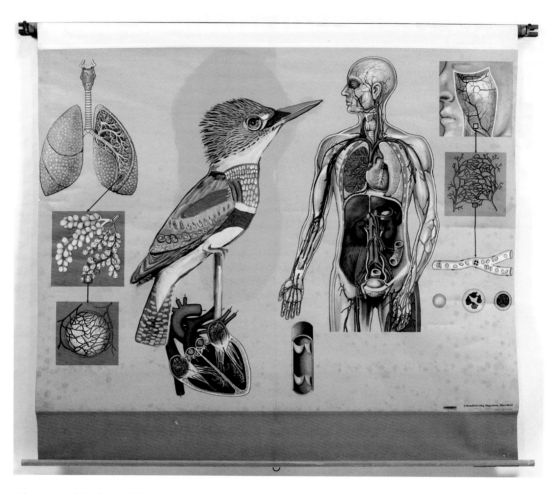

Abstraction with kingfisher, 2003
Acrylic painting on found material, 2003, 53 x 69 1⁄2"

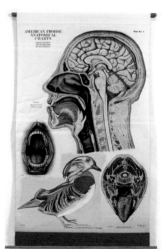

Right: **Abstraction with fancy duck, 2003**
Acrylic painting on found material, 74 x 47"

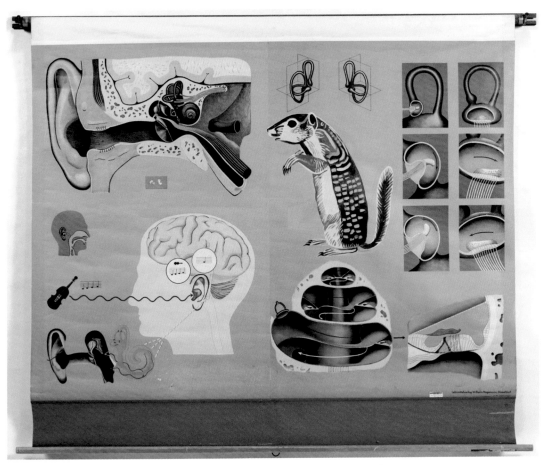

Abstraction with prairie dog, 2003
Acrylic painting on found material, 53 x 69 1/2"

William Jacob Hays
Prairie Dog Village, 1867
Oil on canvas, 36 x 72"
Collection Tweed Museum of Art,
Gift of Mrs. E. L. Tuohy

The Peapod from The Princess and the Pea, 2003
Gouache and watercolor on paper, 23 x 30"

Aspects of the Frog
Prince No. 2, 2003
Gouache and watercolor
on paper, 23 x 30"

A prince is a man in a frog suit.
A woman is a lure in the shape of a hook.
I favor fringe. I favor the soft effect of fabric over steel.
I like pretty hooks and feathers. I like the feminine deal.

The world is a green pool for fishergirls.
The bed is your mollusk, your thirsty shell.
Drink, little fishergirl, drink.
The pool is your heaven and it is your hell.

He will always leap and you will always lure.
A romance is a story in the shape of a hook.
A fishergirl baits her line with a feathery tip.
A fishergirl drags him up from the green pool

into her mollusk bed, into her thirsty shell,
into her heaven or is it her hell?
Think, little fishergirl, think.
You can keep him if you catch him

but you can always let him go.

–Camille Norton

Convenience Food Engineering; Placemats
from Sue's Gene Splice Cafe, 2003
Offset lithography on paper, 10 1/2 x 15"

The work in this section explores issues like genetic engineering, species extinction, and the pervasive use of images of animals, plants and the natural environment as they are transmutated into objects of culture. For the body of work *Reproducing Nature*, Johnson creates traditional-looking illustrations of nature found on the surfaces of everyday objects, with the corresponding objects exhibited next to her paintings. This strategy of analysis by comparison,

so common to science, is also key to her series of *Blueprints* and *Comparative Anatomies*. *Spokesanimals* and *Mutations* from *Unpublished Encyclopedia* put a scientific and cultural spin on, as Johnson says, tongue-in-cheek, the "need to employ wild animals to sell commercial products." American culture has found the innocent animal to be a more trustworthy spokesperson, when compared to the human, who will say anything for a buck. The mass-production of plastic toys representing these animals, often dressed in human clothing, has created a new species of animal that can now be collected and catalogued." Free take-away restaurant placemats from *Sue's Genetic Soup Café* are stacked in front of the watercolor illustrations from *Convenience Food Engineering*, a series of works that humorously proposes new species to make food preparation more - well, convenient!

Convenience Food Engineering; (sole oliveloaffish), 2000-01
gouache and watercolor on paper, 11"x14"

Re-producing Nature
objects collected by
the artist with
corresponding paintings

Re-producing Nature; 2002
gouache and watercolor on paper, 20 x 16"

Top Left:
Shell animals, doggy and bunny

Top Right:
Smiling Florida navel orange

Bottom Left:
Mutant romantic floral ivy

Bottom Right:
Turkey with black and blue checkerboard drumstick legs

Pages from an unpublished
encyclopedia, unknown
origin; 2003
Objects: assorted spokesanimals.
Collection of the artist.

Pages from an unpublished encyclopedia, unknown origin; 2003
Silicone intaglio prints 10 x 7 ½"

Top Left: **Spokesanimals**, page 373

Top Right: **Mutations**, page 241

Bottom Left: **Women Drivers**, page 987

Bottom Right: **Nature's Firefighters**, page 93

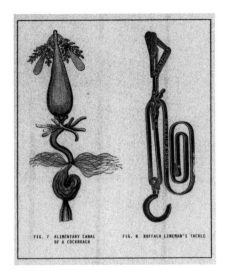

FIG. 7 ALIMENTARY CANAL
OF A COCKROACH

FIG. 8 BUFFALO LINEMAN'S TACKLE

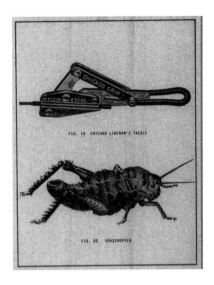

FIG. 19 CHICAGO LINEMAN'S TACKLE

FIG. 20 GRASSHOPPER

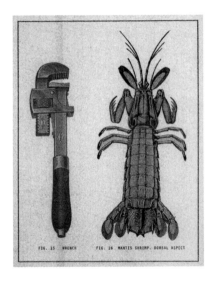

FIG. 15 WRENCH

FIG. 16 MANTIS SHRIMP. DORSAL ASPECT

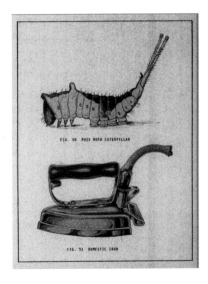

FIG. 50 PUSS MOTH CATERPILLAR

FIG. 51 DOMESTIC IRON

Blueprint of Nature, (Figs 7/8, 19/20, 15/16, 50/51), 2003
Blueprints, 11 x 8.5"

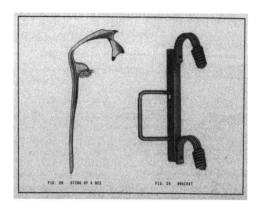

Blueprint of Nature, (Figs 28 29) 2003
Blueprint, 11 x 8.5"

It is everything at once, an arrangement
of parts, a sort of mesh

of like into unlike, same into same,
body into nature, nature into

the picture of nature. Your abstract love
fits me, darling like hand in glove.

Oh let me imitate your tongue and groove,
I want to leave your imprint everywhere,

you as I imagined you and you as you were
in the real where we subsisted, lover and beloved.

But is it love, this imitation I reproduce as wonder,
my desire to compact and compress

your parts against my parts, my desire
to have you whole or anyway configured

as my other part, my mirror?
If I should move, would you move with me?

Would you dance with me? Would you be my shadow?
Would you be everything at once, an arrangement

of parts into my parts, my lover, my beloved,
my sister, my brother, my other, my one?

–Camille Norton

illustration style turkey imprinted on a coffee percolator - reveal the idea that the person responsible for this collection of objects is in fact seeking particular kinds of objects that show manifestations or visualizations of nature. Conversely, the collection of cultured views of nature might be construed as simply a contemporary cross-section of the artifacts of culture. Either way it works. There is another aesthetic and premise at work when objects are collected under the *New Ark* heading, where the collected artifacts are preserved in vacuum-sealed plastic bags like a meal to be frozen for later on. Here the collector is looking for everyday objects - dryer lint, cotton balls, and items from popular culture like stuffed animals or McDonald's ™ Happy Meal toys - and these objects are transformed into quasi-scientific specimens through this preservation process. In the whole of *The Alternate Encyclopedia*, there is a sense of seeing each body of work through a different person's eyes. *Hidden Structures of the Universe* rediscovers a "lost" text presented in such a way that it really looks like it's been a recovered text, when of course it's completely fictitious. It could have been a real text, lost and rediscovered, and the tension operating in that work revolves around how does one know what is missing, until it's rediscovered or recovered. The authentication of the unknown is very much at the heart of my project.

PS You also transform your found objects. The anatomy charts comment on one system of information by inserting new information in a way that makes it seem like it was there in the first place.

SJ Located in the *Cultivating Young Minds* section are the *Abstractions*, large human anatomy charts that I have altered by the addition of overlapping painted images of animals. I call them abstractions because of course schematic information is an abstraction, though we tend to view the images as highly representational and accurate. In the chart representing the digestive system, for

example, the dissected body is digesting a slice of olive loaf. I see cold cuts as the perfect transformative subject-object because a slice can be both macro and micro in alternating moments - at once a view of a planet, then lunch meat, then something unrecognizable. The other important thing about olive loaf, or cold cuts in general in the context of my work is that they are akin to cross-sections of organisms. It's a slice of an animal, but one that has been processed into something non-natural and consumable. I'm very drawn to cross-sections, as a way of exposing things we don't normally see. An alternate way of seeing reality, really.

PS A tried and true strategy of scientific illustration - picturing something dissected, to reveal the mysteries of its interior. Enlarging it, to make it clearer.

SJ My artists book <u>Hidden Structures of the Universe</u> is all about microcosms we cannot see with the naked eye but that reveal and mirror the constructions of our cultural lives. The book rediscovers the lost work of a fictionalized, yet historically possible 19th century female scientist. It brings to light one woman's discovery of the underlying structure of the universe. She comes to understand this structure through the lens of her own experience of being a woman and begins to catalogue and name this world in relation to her lived experience. Thus the "Beaded Bag Diatoms" are shapes quite similar to standard depictions of diatoms and yet in naming them for a female accessory, this particular scientist seeks to reference her own world.

PS So it's not just a matter of what we can't see physically, but also about revealing the information or the perspectives of certain people - in this case the 19th century woman scientist - that culture hides from us. Your works are populated mainly by animals and other organisms - what about their perspective?

SJ Well, for example in the *Abstractions*, I've set up a situation in which a four-foot tall kingfisher bird and a dissected human are regarding each other as if in a painting narrative. Often in my work I like to present the possibility that nature is self-conscious in ways that we humans don't normally assume or only reserve for our own states of consciousness. This series of paintings on the found anatomy charts is also homage to the methods of artist Max Ernst, who used encyclopedic and catalog pages as the basis of many transformative images. There's another altered anatomy chart featuring the diagramming of human hearing with a lone, upright Prairie dog.

PS No doubt inspired by the Tweed Museum of Art's painting *Prairie Dog Village* by William Jacob Hays…

SJ Yes. I was very taken with that work in the collection and wanted to do a piece in response. Prairie dogs are known for sitting up and listening, sensing alarm, and this chart is all about hearing, with practical examples of hearing. The additions and alterations I have made are camouflaged, allowing the viewer the possibility of experiencing the chart as authentic, and only subsequently becoming aware of the alterations. The charts are also about presenting nature in a context that is not only about looking at the human animal, but is more about looking at humans and animals together. Animal zoological information is more often presented without human zoological information, underscoring the idea of nature as other. My project views humans as a part of nature, and unavoidably, nature as part of culture.

PS Your work is full of information, and has the look of authority, and yet the information is not, let's say, the kind you'd want a surgeon to have before operating on you. The entry into the work has to do with our recognition of this information in the guise of authority, in a form we usually believe to be "true". You alter the information, but respect the form, and in doing so, you comment on the form.

SJ Certainly one of the structures of this exhibition and the way it tells its story is through the power of the form. We immediately recognize authoritarian forms like the charts, and understand that it is not a naturalistic representation, but instead like reading a road map. We are accustomed to deciphering the visual codes. By juxtaposing incongruous information - like an oversized bird and a dissected human torso - while still maintaining a sense of authority, my aim is to produce both a rupture of seeing and a poetic sequence. Other bodies of work in the exhibition purposefully adopt a particular technique - like a printmaking or painting technique – to mimic a form that is ultimately very believable. A watercolor that is highly detailed and carefully rendered signals a faithful interpretation of the world around us. A cross-section or an image that shows multiple views signals a veracity which seems to be the result of intense scrutiny of the world, in that the artist-scientist has exhausted herself by viewing the thing from all angles. Detail is often equated with truth. And although we live in an age of rapidly outdated and superseded information, an authoritative "just-the-facts" presentation wins belief. So I try to use the visual form of information dissemination carried out by museum displays and reference manuals to help authenticate my carefully rendered fictions. Because my alternate system is located just on the borders of the implausible, I am always aware that there is a threshold beyond which the illusion comes apart. When the illusion ultimately does come apart, my hope is that the work then pushes the viewer to reinterpret their relationship to and assumptions about this thing called Nature.

PS Part of the illusion is the use of many different, fictional voices, which you position next to "real" scientific voices.

SJ *The Alternate Encyclopedia* is meant to appear as if there are many authors and researchers – many points of view. Diverse and fictitious books are created to comment on a variety of ways of understanding the natural world. For example, one book adopts the process of architectural blueprinting to provide a link to Henry Fox Talbot's groundbreaking 19th century book <u>Pencil of Nature</u>, in which photography was first used to illustrate the world around us in a small but mass produced publication. In my *Blueprint of Nature* works, the paired images suggest clear morphological relationships between organic and inorganic natures by comparing the anatomies of machine tools and zoological specimens. Does form follow function, or does function follow form?

PS Another trope at work in many of these images is sequencing – they present themselves as a series of steps, views, or variations.

SJ Sequencing is very important in terms of how the information is built or deconstructed. Through the various bodies of work, I've tried to keep building in my audience this sense of believing, and it may be some time before the viewer disbelieves everything – or the viewer is looking for things in my work that are believable, and there are lots of things that express truths. Objects that have been loaned from the Minnesota Historical Society, the St. Louis County Historical Society and the UMD Biology Department are real artifacts that help to authenticate the possibility of my own creations. A sense of the surreal is created when real historical objects are displayed out of their original context and then placed into a new set of concerns. What will people think of the hula-hoop in two-hundred years, or a children's game of making plastic insects out of something called goop? Paul Bunyan is a real folk hero, but where does my narrative intersect with and then veer off from the popular tale? With this installation, it is clear that there is a surrealistic sensibility and that it is not completely factual or "realist," although

the language of realism is the vehicle for communication. Embedded in my work is a comment and expose´, if you will, of the authority created by visual and organizational forms, of an A–Z taxonomy as complete and exhaustive, of diagrams and charts as revealing truth, of detailed renderings encouraging trust, et cetera...

PS In the context of an encyclopedia, the authority of the text is certainly one of those cues to belief.

SJ The use of images and text runs throughout my work. For example, we tend to assume that the visual is less significant in learning things like spelling but in the *Free Association Spelling Book* there is an attempt to bring the visual and textual into balance, and using images that are gender biased in favor of young girls. A picture prompts the free association of words to the image, and the visuals are from a particularly feminine or domestic universe – hair accessories, foodstuffs, decorative pins, and so on... Handwritten in pencil, each print fashions a response culled from thesaurus entries for the first word in the associative chain. A hair barrette prompts "control" and a tangle of spaghetti prompts "chaos."

PS Other pieces, like the *Frog Prince,* are based on real yet fantastic texts.

SJ The fairy tale works are done specifically in the style of specimen pages created by court artists like Jan van Kessel, who was commissioned by the collector Rudolph II to document his possessions. Authentic pages featured elaborate collections of rare and exotic creatures, mixing real and mythological animals together in the scientific renderings. At the time it was common to mix what we now consider mythological creatures, like dragons, for instance, with real creatures that could be observed, like insects. Knowing that the historical visual record is often a mixture of fact and fiction, what I've done is to purposefully insert a fictional character or creature within the context of things that actually are observable in the world. I'm offering other ways of knowing popular fairy tales like *The Frog Prince* or *The Princess and the Pea* - and more obscure stories like *The Whale with No Tail*, which is taken from the 1899 picture book by L. Frank Baum, <u>Father Goose</u>. My father used to read us stories from this book, including the one about the whale who swims through the ocean with a bandaged up tail-section, inconsolably weeping over his situation. I wanted to use a baseline of believability or familiarity, and then start looking at these fairy tales, and rendering the frog prince, for example, in ways that make him both believable and not believable.

PS The fairy tale pieces also involve sequencing or a serial process, one of transformation and metamorphosis.

SJ Yes, aspects of the *Frog Prince No. 2* deal quite specifically with metamorphoses. It shows the frog in an earlier state of gestation nearly jumping out of the picture plane, with an enlarged and accurate-looking pupae laying on the ground, and a somewhat imaginary botanical cross-section.

PS Not a scientifically accurate metamorphoses, of course. You've got him going from a pupa to tadpole to prince. Of course that's why we call it a fairy tale - it's clearly a fiction. But you infuse the picture with the language of scientific illustration.

SJ When I re-read fairy tales in preparation for these works I quickly discovered that there are many different versions of the story of *The Frog Prince*, but in all of them the frog is represented as an aggressive character, who, after he helps the princess in the wood, demands that she make good on her promise to befriend him. As he lands - literally - on her doorstep, she is repulsed by his desires and doesn't want him to sleep in her room, and definitely not in her bed.

PS Who could blame her, really?

SJ Right! In the first frog prince piece (No. 1), I wanted to picture a frog that was already in mid-transformation, so in my depiction he appears to be a human/animal combination with a human grin and clammy hands, lasciviously looking to eat this sumptuous and fleshy atlas moth. In my mind, the moth represents the frog's own metamorphosis, and in consuming the moth he destroys evidence of the transformation process. There are also jellyfish forms in the painting, amorphous forms in the upper left and right that take the position of eye sockets in the overall composition. The frog himself becomes the nose and the moth becomes the mouth. I was thinking here of the 16th century painter Guiseppe Archimboldo with his famous series of portraits composed of everything but human flesh - sea creatures, works of literature, seasonal vegetation - so the *Frog Prince No. 1* group of individual specimens metamorphosize into a more threatening image of a salivating head.

PS In your versions of the fairy tales you emphasize the interaction of humans with natural entities, and often these entities are transforming somehow, or assuming a larger than life role in the human character's life. A tiny pea in the *Princess and the Pea* suddenly becomes the element around which the whole story revolves.

SJ It's my way of telling the story so that the pea is the main character, not the princess. Nature as heroine. In so much of my work what I am attempting to show is this parallel sense of reality, of telling the story of interaction between humans and nature. That's where the overarching title of *The Alternate Encyclopedia* comes from - the idea that there is this entirely alternate way that we could be understanding the world, or our place in it.

PS In the case of fictional narratives like fairy tales, the whole idea seems to be that there was or is a "real" story behind or parallel to the fictional

continued on page 31

An ongoing theme in Johnson's work has been the role of women in the sciences, and the definition of "approved" feminine pursuits as arenas of scientific research. As an example, it is now known that many of the natural history plates gracing early encyclopediae were engraved by anonymous women who were never credited for their work. In the book project *Hidden Structures of the Universe* Johnson "discovers" the work of a fictional 19th century female scientist, whose research was never published in her own day. Through the lens of gender, Johnson's fictional scientist comes to the understanding that common forms gird the universe, and that these forms are actually women's undergarments and accessories –for example, "beaded bag diatoms."

The *New Ark* project was inspired by Foodsaver® storage bags, which Johnson saw as a convenient way to store and protect her growing collections of cultural and scientific specimens, but also as a reflection of the "domestic science" to which many aspiring female scientists of the past were relegated. This machine and its process has obvious ties to the preservation of scientific specimens, and to the notion of preservation in museums, the science of cryogenics, and so could easily fall under the headings of New Wonder World, or Wild Animals I Have Known.

Left: **Bird Fan,** n.d.
Baby hawk, 2 x 12 x 9"
Collection of Minnesota Historical Society

Right: **Victorian Hair Wreath**
human hair, braided and knotted, in frames, 14 x 11 x 1"
Collection of St. Louis Country Historical Society

Middle: **Sampler,** n.d.
linen, Queen-stich embroidery with basket and floral motif, 8 x 8"
Collection of Minnesota Historical Society

Right: **Mannequin (woman with ferns),** n.d.
Paper maché, paint, fabric, 20" high
Collection of Minnesota Historical Society

Left: **Sewing Bird,** n.d.
Silver plated, die-stamped metal clamp, 6 x 4 x 2"
Collection of Minnesota Historical Society

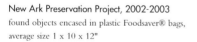

New Ark Preservation Project, 2002-2003
found objects encased in plastic Foodsaver® bags,
average size 1 x 10 x 12"

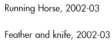

Running Horse, 2002-03

Feather and knife, 2002-03

Laces, 2002-03

Pez dispensers, 2002-03

Dryer lint, 2002-03

Ideal woman, 2002-03

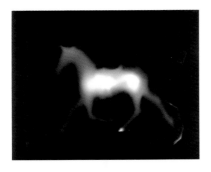

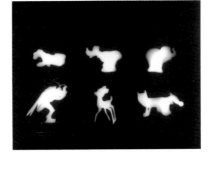

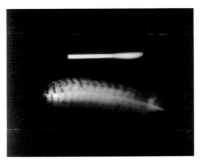

Photograms, 2003
Direct photographic prints of objects in Foodsaver®bags,
each 16 x 20"

Running Horse, 2003

Comparative Anatomy of famous animals, 2003

Comparative Anatomy of knife and feather, 2003

Comparative Anatomy of dryer lint and plastic flowers, 2003

Comparative Anatomy of laces, 2003

Comparative Anatomy of ideal woman and hair sample, 2003

I was in the rapture of the deep with my own kind
and I was floating, floating on a saline tide
inside the lap and flow of pleasure.

I was deep inside the aperture,
an opening of the body and the mind
to the hidden structure. I was in the rapture of the deep.

I was inside the lap and flow of pleasure.
Diatoms sparkled in the nightpools of the sea
and I was a diatom and so was she and we were floating,

floating on a saline tide inside the hidden structure.
I could see the crystalline geometry of the diatom
and of the nightpool and all the stars, the same pattern!

Rock crystal, salt, sand, star, sea, deep in the rapture
of the hidden structure of the body and the mind,
floating, floating inside the lap and flow of pleasure.

–Camille Norton

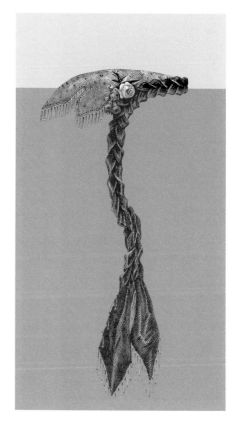

Hidden Structures of the Universe,
Hydromedusa 2001-03
silicone intaglio print

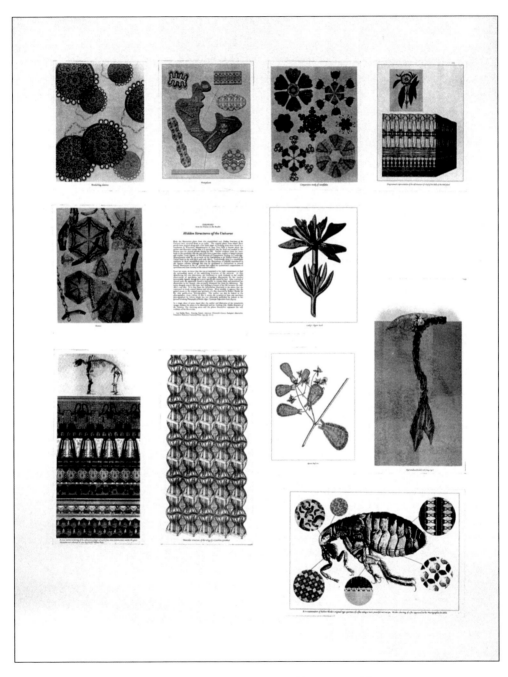

Hidden Structures of the Universe, 2001-03
twelve-plate silicone intaglio print, 50 x 38"

WILD ANIMALS I HAVE KNOWN

35 stuffed tigers. All specimens collected at Amherst, Virginia, July 11, 2003
Collection of the Artist

below: **Myrtle Warbler** specimen in case with painted background, 12 x 14 x 3"
Collection of Department of Biology UMD

A small framed diorama featuring a Myrtle Warbler specimen perched before a painted landscape is a marriage of art and science we expect to find in natural history museums everywhere. In the context of Johnson's work, however, this innocent little bird in its pretty landscape assumes larger-than-life conceptual proportions, because it highlights the dichotomies of falsehood and truth and reality and representation that appear everywhere in her work. The title for this chapter comes from a 1899 illustrated book by Ernst Seton Thompson, which told "true nature stories" for popular audiences.

By "visual autopsy" and scientific cross-sectioning Johnson presents a variety of wild animals that have been "tamed" by culture, either through art, commerce, or science. Our way of "knowing" animals, as Johnson points out, is to dissect, reshape, tame, wear and eat them.
Animals appear throughout the exhibition's five chapters in many forms – as advertising gimmicks, toys, decorative objects, actual scientific specimens – and in Johnson's own cleverly altered illustrations. Her paintings of snakes are "culturally contorted" and given titles reflecting human concepts (eg. Infinity, Meander), while nearby snake specimens borrowed from the UMD Biology Department are similarly re-shaped by their physical containers. In a humorous bit of literal deconstruction, Johnson creates scientific-looking watercolor autopsies of beasts from popular literature – Peter Cottontail, Pegasus, The Ugly Duckling.

Serpentine, 2002
oil on wood panel, 16 x 20"

Infinity, 2002
oil on wood panel, 16 x 20"

Bird and snake specimens
Collection of Department of
Biology, UMD

Katalog, 2003
Color intaglio prints, each 10 x 8"

Shell animals (ventral and dorsal views of doggie and bunny), 2003

Clothespin ducks, 2003

Wooden snowman, 2003

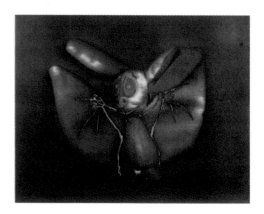

Soft style bat, 2003

Top Left: **Anatomy of Pegasus (Head No. 2), 2003**
gouache and watercolor on paper, 23 x 30"

Top Right: **Anatomy of Pegasus (Head No.1), 2003**
gouache and watercolor on paper, 23 x 30"

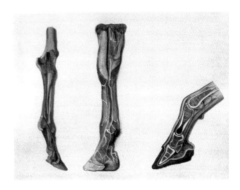

Anatomy of Pegasus (legs and hooves), 2003
gouache and watercolor on paper, 23 x 30"

Anatomy of Pegasus (full view), 2003
goache and watercolor on paper, 23 x 30"

Anatomy of Peter Cottontail with cross-section of
cottontail, 2003
gouache and watercolor on paper, 30 x 23"

So freakish, the immanent beauty of my inside parts,
my pods and coils, my secret life.

The change, they call it: child into girl,
girl into woman, then woman waking ripe

or waxing cold or bursting hot as a chile in the flame
of what the postmoderns call a situation.

My situation's private, like a goiter no one sees.
There's a seed pod swelling in my throat

and I speak differently than I did before the change.
I speak from here, where pressure blooms

out of me like a baby or like a sac
of meaning and what I want to say

is that I am not what I was. I am
a changeling, half-creaturely,

half other-than-creature,
like a mind inside a body

or like a coil inside a girl,
her sleeping snake, her phallic shape

uncoiling into utterance. Come close. Closer.
I want to tell you everything my body knows.

—Camille Norton

Anatomy of the Ugly Duckling, 2003
gouache and watercolor on paper, 30 x 23"

continued from page 19

one. Obviously there's a good "scientific" reason why the frog is used as the animal that transforms into the prince – and that is because of the transformation that frogs actually undergo. They actually do metamorphosize, as do butterflies and moths. They do transform from one physical entity into another, and rather magically.

SJ Morality lessons are often the "reality" that sit behind the mythology or the tall tale. The reader learns to keep two parallel story tracks going as the story progresses, one that follows the literal storytelling and the second that delivers moral guidance.

PS And your works subvert the expected moral, or deflect its delivery.

SJ Yes, for example there is another group of works that propose the scientific study of mythological and fairy tale creatures, suddenly bringing the mythological down to the level of earthly, ordinary science. Pegasus, The Ugly Duckling and Peter Cottontail become the splayed subjects of mundane dissections and autopsies. These works are based on accurate anatomical studies from a late 19th century reference on the comparative anatomy of domesticated animals.

PS So is there a book on the anatomy of mythological creatures?

SJ No – that's the book I'm writing and illustrating! Unlike most of the exhibition, these works attempt to deconstruct the believability of fictions. Alternately they may serve to validate the myth by presenting proof of the existence as a dissected, authentic specimen of science rather than to picture the creature in an artistic rendering complete with Gods and mortals, castles, fluffy clouds and innocent children. I did these in the same time frame as the fairy tale pieces, and I wanted to imbue them with a sense "hard" science crossing over into the world of invention and imagination.

PS That seems to be an overarching metaphor for what you do.

SJ The nature of visual information is different from that of textual information. Today we believe a video or film account over somebody's story of an event. We are fairly discriminating when it comes to literature or a narrative in textual form, but when we see the pictures we want to believe it.

PS The old cliché that "seeing is believing."

SJ That's right. Even in this last century of photographic and digital manipulation, we want to believe. Something about the mirroring of observable "reality" or "experience" is mesmerizing.

PS It may have something to do with the way we store visual information in the brain. I'm sure this could be confirmed, and that there is some research on this, but my understanding in layman's terms is that certain parts of our eyes are made up cells that are just like certain cells in the brain. These cells, I seem to remember, don't regenerate. I am at the "creepy crawler" level in terms of being able to understand the ramifications of this, but I've always wondered if in our visual memory there is some very powerful connection between the eye and the brain at work.

SJ I haven't heard of that, but it's fascinating to think that our eyes might actually be encoding memory as part of a system of capturing and filing visual sensations for future reference. Like storing Polaroid pictures with a time delay for developing…

PS Can we talk about the forms you use? You started as a painter, and you use many different forms of printmaking.

SJ I was trained as a painter, and I did

printmaking while I was in graduate school, but I really didn't do any more printmaking until about ten years later. It was only when I became interested in creating fictitious images and having them seem believable, that I chose to go back into etching, because I saw a relationship between medieval engravings and bestiaries, fiction and belief. At the time I was working on a series of oil paintings that pictured enlarged images of scientific specimens, like a cross-section of a snake head or insect seen through a microscope. What I realized was that while these things were beautiful and seductive, they did not have this believability I wanted. So I turned to printmaking and watercolor, and scaled down the works in order to create a greater suspension of disbelief, which is what I felt needed to happen. If in earlier times a small black and white print could verify the authenticity of a five headed dragon or a mermaid, I wanted to ride on the coattails of that method of creating belief.

PS What you really adopted was the form of the illustrated book.

SJ And the encyclopedia, and the way that knowledge is disseminated through it, came almost immediately and naturally after that. I started working on some of the first pieces that I would consider part of *The Alternate Encyclopedia* as early as 1991, but really didn't understand how I could move it out as a larger project until around 1995.

PS At the same time you adopted the form of the book, it seems as though you also began adopting the form of the museum itself. Both are the locus of collections, both have a sense of authority. Their organization and interpretation by curators, authors, historians and naturalists lends these forms some degree of intellectual power.

SJ Yes, it evolved very naturally, as I was working on the early prints, a group of about forty etchings. I had a residency at the Virginia Center for the Creative Arts. What I began to realize,

having moved from the paintings to the prints, was that using objects together with them lent the prints even more validity. So I began to collect objects and organize them within display cases. Sweet Briar College had a couple of old wooden display cases that were quite lovely, and they lent them to us for a small exhibition. I had a residency for a couple of months, and was able to sort of molt over thinking about how the objects and images worked together. Since that time I've always considered that communal context between the objects and the images.

PS What were some of the first images and objects you paired?

SJ The first objects were intended to help authenticate my prints of fictitious mutated creatures, but actually now I now find them very alarming. I made insects that had all kinds of things glued on to them. A beetle that had lost its head – I found an old bottle stopper that I attached to it. Its identification label said "Stopper head beetle (extremely rare)." Another of my insect constructions was inspired by an actual insect, called the leaf-footed beetle. Its legs mimic leaf forms as a camouflaging device, but what I wanted to do was to create this ironic insect, to call attention to the way that humans name things in such a matter-of-fact way. It was a deadpan sort of joke, but I glued decaying leaves to the end of its legs, so that it would have to drag these completely non-functional leaf-feet along behind it, becoming a leaf-footed beetle in my world. At this point I had started teaching at St. Mary's college of Maryland and a lot of the biologists has taken me under their wing, and had given me aging or broken specimens. One of the biologists had given me this rhinoceros beetle that had a hole where it had been pinned down, and on one of my flea market shopping trips I found a little American flag lapel pin. I didn't want to put another hole in this very delicate beetle carcass, so I decided to put the lapel pin straight down through the existing hole. I called him the "Large American Rhinoceros Beetle." Again, as another play on how we try to identify for different countries these properties, or naming the species after the particular place of origin. So with this little lapel pin the beetle is sporting his identity as an American insect.

PS In the same way that early natural history collecting was a very nationalistic enterprise.

SJ Absolutely. I've done a lot of research, particularly at the American Antiquarian Society. I became very interested in early American science, especially during the time of the New Republic, 1790-1830 or so, when many explorers like Lewis and Clark struck out for the west to find things that held both a great sense of collective mystery and commercial potential, like the true source of the Mississippi or a passage to the East. Many of the naturalists who were part of the expeditions were from Philadelphia, which at the time was a great hub of scientific activity. Both Charles Willson Peale's museum and the American Philosophical Society were there. There was a rush to collect, name and get credit for discoveries in these uncharted regions - it was an era of true bonanza. The rule of the day held that if a discovery was published, even just a few copies, it would then be established as on the record and that person had the right to name the new zoological or botanical find. In the same time period there was considerable tension between Europe and young America. European naturalists had been in America conducting research for their respective countries for many years, collecting, naming, publishing and receiving credit in Europe. After the Revolutionary War, American scientists were of two persuasions. Many wanted to establish themselves and America as a site for credible scientific inquiry, while others who were still tied to the European scientific establishment continued to send documentation of their discoveries back to Europe for publication and what they thought was more authentic validation. It was an intense time of exploration, discovery, and naming, and of trying to possess and impose

order on the New World.

PS So printmaking becomes an essential component of what you do because of its relationship to books, encyclopedias......

SJ ...documentation and dissemination of information, more than one copy going out....

PS And this happens at a time when there have been many artists, from Joseph Kosuth to Fred Wilson, who have been literally "mining" museum collections and looking at the politics of display. What's included and what's not included in collections, how it's interpreted, how it's laid out before the public, what information they're given. The whole notion of museum collections as fodder for artmaking as opposed to being "protected" groups of rarified objects. It's an interesting shift in the way that museums and artists relate to each other.

SJ To whom do we trust the interpretation of information is a vital cultural issue for us right now. When I was living in New York I remember Fred Wilson's work very well, and I am sure that being aware of his work came at the same time that I was beginning this body of work in the early 1990s. And I was certainly aware of Kosuth's work. So the idea that other artists were mining this territory was of great interest to me. There are a lot of artists who are interested in the museum as a site for these kinds of inquiries. In fact, in 1990 Saul Ostrow curated my big specimen paintings into a wide-ranging show about science and display - Mssr. B's Curio Shop at Thread Waxing Space. Maybe he saw some of the latent issues in the work even then.

PS I think the increased involvement of artists, scientists and other cultural workers in the curation of museum collections is very healthy.

SJ Absolutely.

PS There are probably some museum directors and curators who might be a bit nervous about this in some respects, especially in history and science museums. Art museums, on the other hand, may tend to have more flexibility of interpretation, because art has a long tradition of commenting on and critiquing its own subjects. But it hasn't been the norm to take natural history specimens or historical artifacts and documents out of context, and to put them into other personal, societal or critical contexts.

SJ With our current state of information overload at least one thing is becoming clear – there is really no right or wrong path to organizing information. The question is, who has the power and the right to establish a particular system of organization and therefore interpretation? When you have so much information, and accept that it has to be organized by an individual mind, though there may be a sort of collective consciousness about particular directions, every curation is very personal. When a curator in a natural history museum decides to put one animal or specimen next to another, you'd think that it has only to do with the relationship between those specimens in their taxonomies as we traditionally understand them, but sometimes that's just not the case. There can be all kinds of intuitive leaps about how one piece of information is juxtaposed to another. Certainly most natural history curators would attempt to come close to the accepted system at hand and not be whimsical about their juxtapositions, but it's a very quick leap to letting intuition reign when using a visual system of organization. Is it significant when the gaze of one bird meets the gaze of another in a display case of stuffed birds from different families? I've always enjoyed the notion of how creativity enters into science. Einstein was very good about recognizing this when he said, for instance, that "imagination is more important than knowledge' – that one doesn't methodically work out a problem by moving from rational step to rational step.

Instead, truly new ideas come out of some sort of synaptic leap that can't be calculated, that it is very much a matter of intuition and hunches. This may be how ideas like evolution, for instance, came out of non-linear thinking.

PS The most fruitful ideas seem to come out of synthetic thinking as opposed to linear thinking.

SJ This is clearly one of the underlying features of the exhibition itself, this kind of leaping of faith and connecting of information – "It could well have happened this way." This is another way to look at it, if one jumps out of the linear way of thinking.

PS And obviously you are an artist, not a naturalist or a scientist, although you have a lot of experience and knowledge in those areas. Did you do any degree work in the sciences?

SJ No, I didn't, although I've read a lot about art and science, especially early artist-naturalists, and of course looked at a lot of images. In the last ten years while I've been teaching at a small liberal arts college, biologists and colleagues in other disciplines have befriended me, leading me to sources that I have followed up on in my work. Now I wouldn't in any way say I am an expert, but I am much more grounded, so that I have a sense of the history of science and the intersection of visual information and scientific discovery.

PS I think it would be true to say that studies of the history of science are more common today – that a more critical look at how science has developed now exists. There no longer seems to be an assumption that we don't really need to study or critique it because, well, it's science. Leave it alone, it's OK, it's right, it's true. Now we have a sub-field of science that studies sciences itself – its history, its methodologies, the way that scientific information has been collected, organized, stored, written about, and illustrated.

continued on page 39

TRAVEL AND EXPLORATION

Hamm's Beer Sign Advertisement
Molded plastic, with lighted element, 16 x 21 x 6 1/2"
Collection of Minnesota Historical Society

The objects and images in this section offer evidence of how Americans have tamed nature by making travel and recreation in the outdoors more convenient, comfortable and family oriented. Many of these items picture aspects of the "wild" - waterfalls, animals, rugged landscapes - that only 100 years earlier were seen for the first time by non-Native Americans. Reproduced on items like postcards, souvenir plates, pillow covers, and even a ceramic shoe - these objects did and do allow leisure-time travelers to show evidence of their adventuresome journeys.

When Johnson states about Paul Bunyan "chores done - now sightseeing," she refers to a reality of the 1950s, when most old growth forests had been harvested, America was completely mapped and surveyed, new post-war suburbs sprawled, jobs were plentiful, and families, now off the farm, could travel in their affordable new cars. The book project *The Updated Life and Adventures of Paul Bunyan and his Blue Ox Babe* attempts to position the early 20th century advertising myth in a situation that allows them to participate in mid-20th century sightseeing. So often the objects of the tourist gaze themselves, Minnesota's monumental sculptures of Paul and Babe now travel in their fictionalized "retirement," comparing their height to the world's famous monuments.

Americana Jumbos; Clash of the Giant Duck and the Over-grown
Sparrow with Explorers, 2003 Digital inkjet print, 15 x 29"

Americana Jumbos; Deluxe accommodations three blocks from the
monorail, 2003 Digital inkjet print, 15 x 29"

The Updated Life and Adventures of Paul Bunyan and his Blue Ox Babe, 2003, Intaglio prints 7.5 x 10"

Rocketry

Chores done, now sightseeing

Mountie Farewell

Too big for the bus

Pierre The Voyager

St. Basil's Cathedral

She's a big girl, Babe, big as a wilderness
or the Great Plains or the tall pines of Coeur d'Alene, Idaho.
She's buff and strong as any woman or any man
and she's my America, made like me out of the same idea.

Babe's pretty horns curl up like the handlebars of my mustache.
She plants her hoofs and I plant my boots on a fresh landscape
of smoky stumps, new-cut from the interior forest of a Northern plateau.
As I smoke my pipe and regard the effect of a good day's work with an ax,
she regards it too out of her sloe-eye, the eye she turns toward the world.

With an ox like Babe by your side anything's possible and so we travel.
We're too big for the bus. We take the shuttle to Cape Canaveral
to watch the rockets, then venture north to the heart of Venture Capital.
On our way to Europe, we build the Panama Canal.
Babe's got an eye for architecture, likes the sight of skyscrapers,
likes to go first class into the future, into the past.

Together we forge rivers with Pierre the Voyager,
herd buffalo with the Indian Killer, Buffalo Bill.
Many men wanted her but she chose me.
At night, I lie down beside her thick blue fur,
nuzzle her soft snout, and whisper, Babe, Babe.
stay with me. And she stays with me, that's the miracle

of love that we call history. You know the story.
I am a gentle man. She is my wife, my faithful ox.
It is an alternative lifestyle, to be sure.
But who among you dares to judge a love so pure?

—Camille Norton

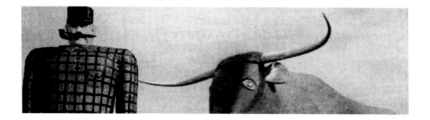

continuted from page 34

Science has become more critical of itself. Also, it now explores its connections to diverse cultures, in the relatively new fields of ethnobotany and ethnomathematics.

SJ Right. One of the things that I collect and that I enjoy enormously, is outdated information. I am constantly going to used bookstores to find texts that fix information that I know is "obsolete" or in other words, "wrong" by contemporary standards. I love to come across information that doesn't jive with other information. This is something that certainly informs my thinking, though I haven't done too many pieces that relate directly to it. At the same time I think that *Hidden Structures of the Universe* is about a specific kind of information that hasn't been granted its validity yet.

PS This idea of outdated or erroneous scientific information reminds me of objects like those found in the "Museum of Questionable Medical Devices, or in the Museum of Jurasic Technology." A lot of those devices were created with clear and serious intentions, to be useful based on the knowledge of their time. But it wasn't long before people discovered that maybe it really wasn't a great idea, for example, to put live wires in their ears.

SJ There are so many examples of questionable practice, and we live in a very litigious environment, which is much more conscious of –for example– gender inequities, but it doesn't take but a dip back twenty years to see how differently we now conceive of the universe. When I was in Worcester at the American Antiquarian Society I made the most fantastic discovery in coming across a suite of 19th century prints by John Fisk Allen documenting the American water lily. A scientific narrative accompanies these oversized prints that explains an experiment carried out to gauge the weight bearing capacity of a lily pad. The scientist (not Allen) decided the perfect way to do this would

be to take his youngest daughter, weighing something like forty pounds, and place her on the lily pad. For counterbalance he put a copper lid weighing something like fifteen pounds on the other side, presumably so his daughter wouldn't simply sink into the water. Now, who knows why he didn't just use two weights of approximately equal weight in this demonstration, but now we can conjure up this picture of a young girl on a giant lily pad, because her father the scientist decided that this was a reasonable way to demonstrate how much weight a giant lily pad can hold. This is even more humorous and disquieting to me because I came across a postcard from the 1950s, that refigures this authentic but idiosyncratic scientific moment, where ayoung girl stands on a giant lily pad at Longwood Gardens in Pennsylvania. It's completely in sync with this earlier experiment. I love this kind of stuff.

PS One of the things you've started working with, not unrelated to printmaking I suppose, is the Foodsaver® bags.

SJ In this instance, two concerns merge together. First, one of the consistent threads running through the project is a commentary and reinterpretation of the history of women and science, and specifically how participation in science was often denied to women. And second, in the last couple of years I have been increasingly aware that my ever-growing collection of strange cultural objects is in danger of being damaged in their storage boxes. In a moment of intuitive leaping, I pondered how a wanna-be scientist-homemaker might preserve her specimens. I just had an immediate notion that these Foodsaver® sealing machines I had seen in TV ads, you know, sucking out the air, compressing the specimen/leftover meal, would be perfect. The appropriation of this common kitchen device attempts to bridge the gap between esoteric scholarly work and the layperson's (especially female) contributions to art and science. The compressed specimens are not typical scientific specimens but can instead be organized into at least two categories: 1) images of "new" nature that have been manufactured – stuffed and plastic toy animals or functional objects with images of nature cast upon them; and 2) everyday banal objects that are often associated with the feminine, but not exclusively – cotton balls, dryer lint, cosmetic sponges, bobbie pins, lentils, Easter grass, and so forth. Because the collected specimens are hermetically preserved in plastic, my ironic hope is that they will survive like diapers in a landfill, and as an aggregate, may come to be understood as the last of their kind by future civilizations – perhaps the best way to archive important scientific specimens.

PS Have you found any other interesting devices to use?

SJ Well, there is the piece "Early Genetic Engineering for Kids, circa 1960s."

PS Also known as "Creepy Crawlers."

SJ I go to a lot of yard sales, flea markets, places like that, and you can learn a lot about a culture by what it throws away. Anytime I come across a lot of any one thing, I say "Hmmm... there was a lot of that out there and now its being discarded – – something else must have replaced it, it's obsolete, but at some point it must have been an important or desirable object." I start formulating a sense of that object as being more or less important in an historical or contemporary moment. It so happened that I was on such a "research excursion" while in residence at the MacDowell Colony, when I came across five sets of these "Creepy Crawler" machines plus some kid's discarded mutant insects at a local yard sale. I remember using one of these machines as a kid. I didn't have one myself, I went over to a friend's house to use it. We'd pour plastic colored goop into molds – sort of like a Frankensteinian thing (thank you Stuart Horodner for curating a show

by that same name) – heat them up in a cooker and make our own bugs. I've done many pieces relating to insects, and as soon as I saw these things I decided to buy them and make bugs myself. It started occurring to me that this object was a really a manifestation of genetic engineering. It was created in the 1960s, as the scientists of today who are pressing forward in the field of genetic engineering were kids, just like me. We had all grown up in an environment where a toy was encouraging us to create new species. "Mr. Potato Head" probably falls into a similar category, though he should also be understood as an effort to demystify nature by assigning human characteristics. To see toys in a new light becomes very important. To understand that play becomes work, and that "scientific play" becomes discovery.

PS Of course there is a lot of controversy around genetic engineering. Its critics often say we are "playing God." So we even use the same terminology.

SJ We have for some time incorporated into our culture the notion that hybridized or genetically altered products is our goal. Better living through technology. The controlled hybridizing of plants started well over one-hundred years ago with Mendel's genetic experiments with plants, and even earlier if one considers the 17th century tulip craze in The Netherlands. There is a long history of doing this, and yet I don't think we look back and see how long a tradition humans have of manipulating nature. That is another one of the threads that runs throughout the entire exhibition.

PS *The Alternate Encyclopedia* is set up in a series of installations that have prints, watercolors, drawings, things one might expect to see in an art exhibition, and then cases full of related material that responds to the imagery in the two-dimensional work. Is it fair to say that you as a collector are making art as a response to what you've discovered and collected?

SJ Yes, it's very fair to say that. I had a revelation a while back, which is that I actually don't respond well as an artist to phenomenon in front of me - to actually being in nature, seeing a bug crawl on the ground. That I in fact have my "authentic moment" in relationship to the artifact. The picture book. The discarded object. I find myself being more interested in and more responsive to an illustration created by someone else that is documenting information that I cannot see for myself.

PS Maybe that's part of the difference between an artist and a scientist today, is that the response is not to the first hand stimuli, but to something that has already been mediated.

SJ I like that idea. And one of the things that becomes clear in my larger *oeuvre* - for example the paintings I do that are related to *The Alternate Encyclopedia* project, yet are distinct, is that those oil paintings are responding to artifacts. So when I picture a particular animal, it's from an image I have seen in reproduction, not in reality. So I am living in this world of artifact and document. Audubon would often sign his drawings with his name and then add "drawn from life." This was a real misnomer in a way because often he killed the birds in order to pose and draw them. When he said "from life," he meant that they had been alive and he was trying to recreate this sense of aliveness that he had seen. But further than that, there is ample evidence from a terrific essay by Linda Dugan Partridge that Audubon based many of his works on drawings created by previous artists. He used the visual models as a starting point, and then augmented the information with what he observed in the wild. The history of natural history illustration is filled with artists who are not exactly copying after nature; they are not looking at something that's live, or even a dead specimen. It was a common practice to copy an earlier illustration, which itself might have

been a copy of a previous illustration, and so forth. And so this game of telephone happens when artists copy artists who have copied artists. In our contemporary time, we hold on to the virtue that originality and individuality are important, but of course that hasn't always been the case in the past.

PS Your homage to Albrecht Durer's *Rhinoceros* is a case in point.

SJ Most certainly. One of the early lightning rods for *The Alternate Encyclopedia* was a print I based on the Durer *Rhinoceros* of 1515. The story goes something like this: there was a rhinoceros and I believe an elephant that were being brought by ship to Portugal destined for the royal zoo, and there had not been a rhinoceros seen in Europe before then, so there was much anticipation about this animal coming. Tragically the ship sinks off the coast and the animals are lost. All that remains is a quick sketch and a written description by one of the ship's crew in which the rhinoceros is described to have protruding horns, skin like armor plating and a very aggressive disposition. A sought-after artist, Durer is commissioned to make a print of this animal he has never seen. As soon as a print is made of this exotic creature and the "news" is disseminated, just like a photo in a tabloid or a scandalous video on TV today, the print is consumed culturally. Everyone wants a copy of this print but of course only so many are made, so what happens over the next 250 years is that the print is copied and recopied, and finds its way into encyclopedias, disseminated like a photo, or better yet, clip-art would be today, or like jpeg files through the Internet. As artists continue to copy and recopy Durer's print, the information is degraded, and the way that it degrades is interesting, because it magnifies and multiplies Durer's guesswork and exaggerations, which were the result of his working without direct reference. By an early 18th century encyclopedia the descendants of Durer's rhinoceros actually look like little armored tanks. As a way of acknowledging both my process and the processes of previous artists, I created a rendition of the creature myself, except I carried the transformation a bit further by adding medieval armor and gauntlets onto the beast to replace his legs. This is a perfect example of how information is both superseded and yet remains an authentic artifact in the visual and scientific record.

PS And then there is the introduction of photography and the idea of photographic truth. When you can create an image without the intervention of the human hand, evidence of its truth become irrefutable.

SJ One would think. But of course this is not true, because photographs have been doctored from the very beginning.

PS You mean those UFO photographs are not true?

SJ I love those! I've done a few pieces over the years related to UFOs – this phenomenon of a cultural paranoia that something like a UFO could actually be there. After my grandmother passed away I found a newspaper clipping of a supposed UFO over which she matter-of-factly wrote in red pen, "just like the one I saw."

PS Your Paul Bunyan pieces seem to play at or with the edges of photographic "truth."

SJ I'm very inspired by the story of Paul Bunyan and how it lays the foundation for a contemporary sensibility about possessing and controlling nature. Inspired by the Bemidji monuments, The *Updated Life and Adventures of Paul Bunyan and His Blue Ox Babe* chronicles their lives only after their lumberjacking chores are done. And as the narrative reveals, like so many Americans with more leisure time, Paul and Babe decide to set off on a sightseeing adventure to visit other famous larger-than-life monuments, including the Empire State Building, the Pyramids and the Leaning Tower of Pisa. Along the way they pose for vacation snapshots that serve as "proof" of their relative size in relation to dinosaurs, giant turtles, boys on stilts, and so forth.

PS You might be interested to know that Paul and Babe did recently move from their long-time home in downtown Bemidji, Minnesota, to a small park outside that town. And now you've sponsored their virtual travel worldwide, letting them be the tourists for a change. I am sure they appreciate that, having been the subject of millions of tourist snapshots where they were forced to be the monument.

SJ It's shocking to hear that Paul and Babe are "on the move" – it's clearly another case of life imitating art, or mythology imitating art, or something like that! And as you say, I tried to give them an alternate life path through the series of documents from their sightseeing adventures. I tend to like photographic information that is mass-produced, like the postcard because it is simultaneously a great indicator of popular opinion and consumerism, and oddly often exhibits passages of unfocused or degraded information. Also in the *Travel and Exploration* chapter along with Paul and Babe are some oversize jumbo postcards, measuring about 20" across. I wanted to call attention to the souvenir as proof of exploration while at the same time use the "super-sized" American culture mentality that bigger is better. Digitally manipulated composite images scanned from my own postcard collection, these new images are overloaded with vistas of unexplored and untamed nature opening up just outside one's motel door or outside the window of a scenic touring vehicle. In one postcard image, the impossible view of the Matterhorn is seen spliced together with a run-on sentence of American hotels and motels with their swimming pools and skating rinks ready to make it easy for the tourist to experience nature's splendor.

PS There has always been a fascination with

trying to capture the enormity of nature in art, but the reality of it is that you capture very little of it, even with a veristic documentary photograph.

SJ A camera sees far less than the eye sees. There exists a notion that a camera is going to record reality, and many people accept that notion. But again, it's a viewpoint, and a photograph can leave out as much as it includes. I love the conflict between those things. The photographic process is included in the exhibition, with the photograms that document objects preserved in the Foodsaver® bags. I wanted to create an authentic document of a fictitious document.

PS It's interesting that almost as soon as photography is established, artists begin to manipulate it. In other words, there's really no deep trust in photography to begin with that it tells us anything we don't already know, or can't see with our own eyes. Maybe stop-action photography, like Eadweard Muybridge's sequential photos of the human figure and animals in motion, might be an interesting new...

SJ ...scientific approach

PS But right away you have artists manipulating the photographic image.

SJ I think that the people who were really interested in composing visual images were some of the people who were developing early photographic processes. I team-taught a course with my colleague in photography, Colby Caldwell, on the relationship between painting and photography from those early days right up through the recent David Hockney debates. I find Hockney's overall proposal very compelling. I think he's on to something that is tremendously important art historically and in terms of the relationship between photography and what we consider to be photographic, going back to the camera obscura. In the 1840s, this was when

painting was first declared "dead," because the photograph was going to eliminate the need to have an artist render an oftentimes quite subjective likeness. At the time, and in the face of a growing culture and embrace of science, subjectivity was out and objectivity was in. Or so it seemed initially.

PS I think it's closer to the truth that we really don't want that objectivity.

SJ Ultimately, yes, that's true. Darkroom manipulation of photographs starts almost immediately in the history of photography. There is a group of early photographers who wanted their work to be understood in a fine art context and actually started working with darkroom processes as if they were manipulating materials in a painting studio. Today we might be more aware of the techniques of image manipulation but that doesn't stop us from casting intrigued glances at bizarre pictorial tabloid covers at the supermarket checkout. "Seeing is believing." "A picture is worth a thousand words." Even though I am very aware of my own mistrust of the evidence, the artifact, it is still very compelling when confronted with a photograph. It's very deeply embedded in our culture.

PS It is, and I think that we do respond differently in a physiological sense to photographic imagery, as opposed to sculpture or a painting. We are being given something that we could have seen ourselves with our own eyes, had we been behind the same lens at that same moment. We tend not to question it too much.

SJ That's right. And I think that's because most of us are pretty unconscious photographers if you will, with the snapshot. Anyone who's taken a few photographs knows that whether you're standing or sitting... if you come up close to something, depth of field... you can make things out of proportion very easily or exclude things from the frame of reference that our peripheral vision would pick up, and that might completely alter the portrayal of information. But because photographs come closer to mimicking what we seem to perceive of the world, arresting time in the process, without the apparent intervention of he artist's "hand," wholesale belief is not far behind. More and more I come to believe it's this sense of stopping time, which we cannot do ourselves and which doesn't mirror our reality, that gives a photograph its power over us, and not the mirroring of "reality."

PS And yet again, and we talked about this generationally, we now have 3rd graders who are adept at manipulating photographs on the computer, scanning images of themselves in and placing them in places where they never were or never would be.

SJ Again, this whole morphing thing. The fact that morphing is even a word in the popular vocabulary amazes me. I remember when people first started using the word. It should be a scientific term, but instead it's a popular notion about how one juxtaposes and transforms information and matter. And obviously very related to genetic engineering.

PS But it's also a media issue and a commercial issue. It's about how to transform yourself by merging with some other thing, be it a product, a certain kind of person or activity. There's a company that produces clothing for snowboarders which is actually called Morphic®, and the clothing actually transforms in the sense that you can peel or zip the sleeves and legs off to reveal a different color, or take part of the clothing off and zip it on to something else. It can change its appearance and its function.

SJ Wow! But how is that different from the plastic peel-off game of Colorforms I remember as a kid, where you could dress the background doll or compose a landscape with different collage pieces? Or how is it different from having a physical doll, and dressing it in different clothes?

PS It really isn't different, but these aren't dolls, they are living people. This notion of morphing is very pronounced in our culture. I think the reason for it, beyond the idea of evolving fashion, is that there's a lot of money in it. From cartoons to computer video games, to soft drinks to clothing, to youth culture sports like skateboarding, BMX and snowboarding. Morphing is part of promoting a youth culture, and it becomes part of the marketing of goods to that audience, where market analysts tell us there is a lot of money to be spent.

SJ There is no question that the younger generation today is incredibly fluid in the way that they understand reality. Reality is not fixed. We may talk 'till we're blue in the face about the post-modern, but they're living it, and they haven't known anything different. That's one of the things that becomes a challenge in teaching, the self awareness that they are in the post-modern state, as we older generation folks have attempted to define it, is very difficult to discuss with them because they don't have an alternate reality with which to compare their contemporary state of being.

PS How do you touch base with people if you don't know where the base is.

SJ Right. Or if you haven't experienced something that is fixed, how can you understand the non-fixed? I think that's what I experience.

PS And yet in terms of art, this notion of experimentation with impermanence has been around for a while. Surrealism and Dada, experiments with artmaking from the subconscious. Cezanne's perceptual experiments, Picasso and analytical cubism, Duchamp's "Nude Descending a Staircase" - the idea of showing multiple viewpoints and motion. Visual descriptions of a non-fixed reality, in sync with newly minted scientific notions of relativity - this all seems related to contemporary concepts of morphing.

SJ It's all there.

FLANKED BY TREES, this UFO was photographed in Albuquerque, N. Mex., in June, 1963. The picture is in the U.S. Air-Force's Project Blue Book.

Newspaper Clipping found among the effects of the artist's grandmother, with handwritten inscription: "Just like what I saw."

EXHIBITION CHECKLIST

(All works collection of the artist unless otherwise indicated; dimensions listed are h x w x d in inches.)

INTRODUCTION

Self-Portrait as an artist-naturalist, Loplop's Sister
(after Max Ernst), 2000-01
oil on linen, 38 x 50"
Collection of Tweed Museum of Art, University
of Minnesota Duluth, Sax Purchase Fund

The Last Buffalo (red velvet chair with buffalo horns),
n.d. (ca. early 20th c.)
buffalo horns, red velvet over wood,
Collection of St. Louis County Historical Society,
Duluth, MN

Prairie Chicken (Tynpanuchus cupido)
taxidermied bird specimen
Collection of Department of Biology, University
of Minnesota Duluth

CULTIVATING YOUNG MINDS

Vintage school desk-chair, ca. 1950s
Wood, metal, 31 x 33 x 24"

Free Association Spelling Book, 2002-03
Unique prints, relief and Xerox-transfer with
pencil, 17 x 18" each
Compact
Difference
Incomplete
Screen
Grip
Disorder
Hold
Ideal
Circle
Control

Early Genetic Engineering for Kids
"Creepy Crawlers®" toy, circa 1960's: cooker
unit, two metal molds, two plastic bottles of goop,
specimen display box with plastic insects

Abstraction with prairie dog, 2003
Acrylic painting on found material, 53 x 69 1/2"

Abstraction with olive loaf , 2003
Acrylic painting on found material, 53 x 69 1/2"

Abstraction with fancy duck, 2003
Acrylic painting on found material, 74 x 47"

Abstraction with kingfisher, 2003
Acrylic painting on found material, 53 x 69 1/2"

Aspects of the Frog Prince No. 1, 2003
Gouache and watercolor on paper, 23 x 30"

Aspects of the Frog Prince No. 2, 2003
Gouache and watercolor on paper, 23 x 30"

The Peapod from The Princess and the Pea, 2003
Gouache and watercolor on paper, 23 x 30"

The Whale with No Tail from Father Goose, 2003
Gouache and watercolor on paper, 23 x 30"

The Sawhorse from Oz of Emerald City, 2003
Gouache and watercolor on paper, 23 x 30"

Aspects of Pinocchio, 2003
Gouache and watercolor on paper, 23 x 30"

BOOKS

The Book of Knowledge, Vol. IX, Grolier Society,
Inc. New York, 1949

Ernest Seton Thompson, Wild Animals I Have
Known, Charles Scribner's Sons, New York, 1899

The Wonder of Life, Vol. 10 from The New
Wonder World: A Library of Knowledge, Geo. L.
Shuman & Co., Chicago, 1934

Compton's Pictured Encyclopedia, Vol. 2, F.E.
Compton & Company, Chicago, 1936

The Golden Book of Science for Boys and Girls:
An Introduction to Earth, Sea, the Air, Plants,
Animals, Man and His Inventions, Golden Press,
New York, 1956

Zoological Society Bulletin, Vol. XXIX, No. 1,
January - February, 1926

Collier's Cyclopedia of Social and Commercial Information and Treasury of Useful and Entertaining Knowledge, compiled by Nugent Robinson, P.F. Collier, New York, 1883

The World Book Encyclopedia, Vol. 13, Field Enterprises Educational Corporation, Chicago, 1959

The Insects, Life Nature Library, Time Incorporated, New York, 1962

Richard's Topical Encyclopedia, Volume 2, J.A. Richards Publishing Co., Inc. New York, 1947

Edward S. Holden, Real Things in Nature: A Reading Book of Science for American Boys and Girls, The Macmillan Company, New York, 1913

The National Encyclopedia for Home, School and Library, Vol. 1, National Encyclopedia Company,
Alfred H. Miles, Natural History with Anecdotes, Dodd, Mead & Company, New York, 1895

Everybody's Encyclopedia for Everyday Reference, Charles Morris, Ed., 1907

Our Environment: How We Use It and Control It, Allyn and Bacon, New York, 1945

NEW WONDER WORLD

Convenience Food Engineering: Placemats from Sue's Gene Splice Cafe, 2003
Offset lithography on paper, 10 1/2 x 15"

Convenience Food Engineering: Tasty John Doree fish with savory bacon strip tail, 2000-01
gouache and watercolor on paper, 11 x 14"

Convenience Food Engineering; Hungry-man dinner (Super Jumbo Quad Claw Crab with side dish of red beans), 2000-01
gouache and watercolor on paper, 11 x 13"

Convenience Food Engineering; (soleoliveloafish), 2000-01
gouache and watercolor on paper, 11 x 14"

Re-producing Nature, 2002
gouache and watercolor on paper, each 20 x 16"
Turkey with black and blue checkerboard drumstick legs
Smiling Florida navel orange
Flat-style tortoise
Kingfisher in a landscape with horizon distortion
Mutant romantic floral ivy
Shell animals (doggie and bunny)
Miniature exhibition turkey
Birddog

Re-producing Nature, found objects, variable sizes
Turkey with black and blue checkerboard drumstick legs (coffee pot)
Smiling Florida navel orange (cup)
Flat-style tortoise (carved tortoise shell)
Kingfisher in a landscape with horizon distortion (metal tin)
Mutant romantic floral ivy (decorative wooden plaque)
Shell animals (doggie and bunny)
Miniature exhibition turkey (ceramic figurine)
Birddog (coaster)

Unpublished encyclopedia, Spokesanimals and mutations
Found objects, variable sizes:
Little Sprout figure
Snowman, Dairy Queen figure
Joe Camel mug holder
Tony the Tiger lunchbox
Tony the Tiger stuffed animal
Nestle's Quik Bunny
Catdog
Budweiser Clydesdale
Child-bunny figurine
Human-bird ceramic figurine
Trix, Cocoa Puffs, Honey-nut Cheerios cereal boxes

Pages from an unpublished encyclopedia, unknown origin, 2003
Silicone intaglio prints, each 10 x 7 1/2"
Travel in America, page 465

Hybrids, page 117
Women Drivers, page 987
Nature's Firefighters, page 93
Silicone intaglio prints, 10 x 7 1/2"
Mutations, page 241
Spokesanimals, page 373
Spokeselements Spoons, page 371
Mutations, page 232

Blueprint of Nature, 2003
blueprints on paper, 11 x 8.5"
Figs. 32 & 33
Figs. 36 & 37
Figs. 7 & 8
Figs. 19 & 20
Figs. 30 & 31
Figs. 17 & 18
Figs. 15 & 16
Figs. 51 & 52
Figs. 5 & 6
Figs. 9 & 10
Figs. 23 & 24
Figs. 26 & 27
Figs. 28 & 29

SCIENTIFIC AMERICAN WOMAN

Hidden Structures of the Universe, 2001-03
twelve-plate silicone intaglio print, 55 x 42"

Hidden Structures of the Universe (artists book),
2001-03
digital inkjet prints in bound book, 9 1/4 x 7 5/8"

Mannequin (woman with ferns), n.d.
Paper mache, paint, fabric, 20" high
Collection of Minnesota Historical Society

Victorian hair wreaths, n.d.
human hair, braided and knotted 14 x 11 x 1"
Collection of St. Louis County Historical Society

Young Girl's Bug Collection, circa 1890's
Embroidery hoop, cloth, insects, 2 x 10 x 11"

Sewing Bird, n.d.
Silver plated, die-stamped metal clamp, 6 x 4 x 2"
Collection of Minnesota Historical Society

Bird fan, n.d.
Baby hawk, 2 x 12 x 9"
Collection of Minnesota Historical Society

Sampler, n.d.
linen, Queen-stitch embroidery with basket and
floral motif, 8 x 8"
Collection of Minnesota Historical Society

*The New Concise Practical Pictorial Companion, Vol.
10, Sewing-Machine Tuesday*, 2002
Silicone intaglio prints, 7 x 5" each

*The New Concise Practical Pictorial Companion, Vol.
3 Catkeychains Crochet*, 2002
Silicone intaglio prints, 7 x 5" each, 2002

New Ark Preservation Project, 2002-03
found objects encased in plastic Foodsaver® bags,
average size 1 x 10 x 12"

Photograms, 2003
Direct photographic prints of objects in
Foodsaver® bags, each 16 x 20"
Comparative Anatomy of a snakeskin
and pantyhose
Comparative Anatomy of famous animals
Comparative Anatomy of laces
Comparative Anatomy of rotary wheel and spiral
Comparative Anatomy of clothespin ducks
Comparative Anatomy of ideal woman
and hair sample
Running Horse
Woman and Caveman
Squirrel, man and woman

WILD ANIMALS I HAVE KNOWN

Snake in a Tube
Coral snake in glass tube,
Collection of Department of Biology, University
of Minnesota Duluth

Snake in a Jar
Cobra snake in glass jar, 12 x 6"
Collection of Department of Biology, University
of Minnesota Duluth

Myrtle Warbler diorama
Taxidermied bird with painted landscape,
12 x 14 x 3"
Collection of Department of Biology, University
of Minnesota Duluth

Red-winged blackbird
Taxidermied bird in plastic cylinder,
6 1⁄2 high x 2" diameter
Collection of Department of Biology, University
of Minnesota Duluth

Serpentine, 2002
oil on wood panel, 16 x 20"

Meander, 2002
oil on wood panel, 20 x 16"

Contortionist, 2002
oil on wood panel, 16 x 20"

Infinity, 2002
oil on wood panel, 20 x 16"

35 stuffed tigers (all specimens collected at
Amherst, Virginia, July 11, 2003)
Toy stuffed animals in vitrine

Anatomy of Pegasus (full view), 2003
gouache and watercolor on paper, 23 x 30"

Anatomy of Pegasus (Head No. 1), 2003
gouache and watercolor on paper, 23 x 30"

Anatomy of Pegasus (Head No. 2), 2003
gouache and watercolor on paper, 23 x 30"

Anatomy of Pegasus (legs and hooves), 2003
gouache and watercolor on paper, 23 x 30"

*Anatomy of Peter Cottontail with cross-section of
cottontail*, 2003
gouache and watercolor on paper, 30 x 23"

Anatomy of The Ugly Duckling, 2003
gouache and watercolor on paper, 30 x 23"

Katalog, 2003
Color intaglio prints, each 10 x 8"
Shell animals (doggie and bunny)
Shell animals (ventral and dorsal views of doggie
and bunny)
Fancy bunny
Fancy duck
Clothespin ducks
Wooden snowman
Soft style bat

TRAVEL AND EXPLORATION

Mountie memorabilia: Mountie Barbie, ceramic
figurine, postcards, beer advertisement
Collection of Tweed Museum of Art, University
of Minnesota Duluth, Gifts of Karal Ann Marling

Hamm's Beer Sign Advertisement
Molded plastic, with lighted element,
Collection of Minnesota Historical Society

Various souvenir objects:
Ceramic lady's shoe with waterfall
Souvenir plates
Florida dolphin snow globes
Red plastic U.S. pencil box
Car bingo game card
Assorted travel brochures and postcards
Arizona Highways magazines

*Americana Jumbos; Clash of the Giant Duck and the
Over-grown Sparrow with Explorers*, 2003
Digital inkjet print, 15 x 29"

Americana Jumbos, Deluxe accommodations three blocks from the monorail, 2003
Digital inkjet print, 15 x 29"

The Updated Life and Adventures of Paul Bunyan and his Blue Ox Babe; 2003
Intaglio prints, each 7 1/2 x 10"
Pierre The Voyager
Too big for the bus
Mountie farewell
Boys on stilts
Relative size of a giant turtle
Empire State Building
Dinosaur
Buffalo Bill
Panama Canal
Leaning tower of Piza
Pyramids
Rocketry
St. Basil's Cathedral

Sue Johnson

Born   San Francisco, California, 1957. Lives and works in Lexington Park, MD.

Education:

> Columbia University, New York, New York, M.F.A. Painting, 1981.
> Syracuse University, Syracuse, New York, B.F.A. Studio Arts, 1979.
> Syracuse University in London in conjunction with Saint Martin's School of Art, 1977-78.
> Syracuse University in Florence, 1978.
> Randolph-Macon Woman's College, 1975-76.

Individual Exhibitions:

> 2004   Tweed Museum of Art, University of Minnesota Duluth, Duluth, MN.
> 2003   Emory University, Schatten Gallery, Atlanta, GA.
> 2002   Midwest Museum of American Art, Elkhart, IN.
> 2001   McLean Project for the Arts, McLean, VA.
> 2000   Hollins University, Roanoke, VA.
> 2000   Jan Cicero Gallery, Chicago, IL.
> 2000   Munson Williams Proctor Institute, School of Art Gallery, Utica, NY.
> 1999   Bucknell Art Gallery, Bucknell University, Lewisburg, PA.
> 1998   Maryland Art Place, Baltimore, MD.
> 1998   The Delaware Center for the Contemporary Arts, Wilmington, DE.
> 1997   School 33 Art Center, Baltimore, MD.
> 1997   Boyden Gallery, St. Mary's College of Maryland, St. Mary's City, MD.
> 1996   Anderson Gallery, Virginia Commonwealth University, Richmond, VA
> 1995   The Virginia Center for the Creative Arts, Sweet Briar, VA.
> 1995   Artists Space at Dance Theater Workshop, New York, NY.
> 1994   Nancy Drysdale Gallery, Washington, D.C.
> 1993   RCCA: The Art Center, The Rensselaer County Council for the Arts, Troy, NY.
> 1985   Patrick King Contemporary Art, Indianapolis, IN.
> 1985   Alverno College, Milwaukee, WI.
> 1985   431 Gallery, Indianapolis, IN.
> 1984   Columbus Cultural Art Center, Columbus, OH.
> 1984   Contemporary Art Workshop, Chicago, IL.
> 1984   Artlink Contemporary Artspace, Fort Wayne, IN.
> 1983   The Pennsylvania State University, Zollar Gallery, University Park, PA.
> 1982   Syracuse University, Syracuse, NY.

Group Exhibitions (Selected):

2002   Insecta Magnifica, curated by Jennifer McGregor, Glyndor Gallery, Wave Hill, Bronx, NY
Neo-naturalism, Orange Art Center, Orange, VA
The Nature of Nature curated by Jeffrey Carr, Boyden Gallery, St. Mary's College of
Maryland, St. Mary's City, MD
Temporal Transformation: A Printmaking Invitational. University of Montana, Missoula, MN
Built by Hand: the Book as Art, Pyramid Atlantic, Riverdale, MD
Small Packages, Cumberland Gallery, Nashville, TN
Artscape, Knoxville Museum of Art, Knoxville, TN

2001   Botanica: Contemporary Art and The World of Plants, University of Delaware,
       Newark, DE
       Summer Invitational, The Painting Center, New York, NY
       Arts in Embassies Program, U.S. Embassy, Papua New Guinea
       Pierogi Flat Files, Brooklyn, NY

2000   ArtScape, Maryland Institute College of Art, Decker Gallery, Baltimore, MD
       Meat Products, Trans Hudson Gallery, New York, NY

1999   Botanica: Contemporary Art and the World of Plants, organized by the Tweed
       Museum of Art, University of Minnesota, Duluth, MN, curated by Peter Spooner
       and travels throughout 1999-2001: Chicago Cultural Center, Chicago, IL; Kresge
       Art Museum, Michigan State University, East Lansing, MI; Tarble Arts Center,
       Eastern Illinois University, Charleston, IL; Plains Art Museum, Fargo, ND;
       Alexandria Museum of Art, Alexandria, LA; Carleton College, Northfield, MN;
       University Galleries, Illinois State University, Normal, IL; Western Gallery, Western
       Washington University, Bellingham, WA.

1998   Prime Focus, curated by Greg Bowen, University Galleries,
       Illinois State University, Normal, IL
       Curio Cabinet of Hybrid Possibilities curated by Andrea Pollan,
       Rockville Arts Place, Rockville, MD
       Food Matters curated by Saul Ostrow and Stuart Horodner,
       Bucknell University, Lewisburg, PA
       Food Matters curated by Saul Ostrow and Stuart Horodner, ES Vandam,
       New York, NY,
       Faculty Art Exhibition, St. Mary's College of Maryland, Boyden Gallery,
       St. Mary's City, MD

1997   Frankensteinian, curated by Stuart Horodner, Caren Golden Gallery, New York, NY
       The Sense of Touch, curated by April Vollmer, Ceres Gallery, New York, NY
       Bradley National Print and Drawing Exhibition curated by Barry Blinderman,
       Bradley University, Peoria, IL

1996   Frankenstein (in Normal) curated by Stuart Horodner, University Galleries, Illinois
       State University, Normal, IL
       Inner Landscapes curated by Karen Wilkin, Gallery One, Toronto,
       Ontario, Canada
       Works on Paper Invitational, Blue Mountain Gallery, New York, NY

1995   Environs, curated by Sarah Tanguy, St. Mary's College of Maryland,
       St. Mary's City, MD

1994   Gallery Group Show, Nancy Drysdale Gallery, Washington, D.C.
       The Press: A Print Workshop, Horodner-Romley Gallery, New York, NY

1993   Charcoal Drawings: Cotton, Johnson and Sheehan, Jill Newhouse Gallery, New York, NY
A Moment Becomes Eternity: Flowers as Image curated by Michael Walls, Bergen Museum of Art and Science, Paramus, NJ
The Return of the Cadavre Exquis, The Drawing Center, New York, NY
Songs of Retribution curated by Nancy Spero, Richard Anderson Gallery, New York, NY
Recent Paintings, St. Mary's College of Maryland, St. Mary's City, MD

1992   Nature Fabrilis curated by Deven Golden, Steibel Modern, New York, NY
Mssr. B's Curio Shop curated by Saul Ostrow, Thread Waxing Space, New York, NY
Morphologic curated by Holly Block, Art in General, New York, NY
Beyond Nature: Paintings by Beverly Fishman, Sue Johnson and Drew Lowenstein, Marymount Manhattan College, MMC Gallery, New York, NY
Painting curated by Steven Salzman, Proctor Art Center, Bard College, Annandale on-Hudson, NY

1991   Entr'acte, Michael Walls Gallery, New York, NY
Triangle Artists' Workshop 1991 Exhibition, Bennington College, Usdan Gallery, Bennington, VT
Still-Alive: Contemporary Still-life Painting curated by Barbara Morris, Rockford College, Rockford College Art Gallery, Rockford, IL
Benefit Exhibition, White Columns, New York, NY

1990   Vital Signs: Artists Respond to the Environment curated by April Vollmer, Henry Street Settlement, NY, NY,
"The Environment Show" curated by April Vollmer, Krasdale Art Gallery, Bronx, NY

1989   Works on Paper curated by Charlotta Kotik, Salena Gallery, Long Island University, Brooklyn, NY
"Small Scale", Parsons School of Design, New York, NY
"Boundaries: A Tradition of Drawing at Herron School of Art", Herron School of Art, Indianapolis, IN

1988   Benefit Exhibition, White Columns, New York, NY

1987   Nu- Nature Again curated by Bill Arning White Columns, New York, NY
Soho Center for Visual Artists, New York, NY

1986   24 x 24, Ruth Siegel Gallery, New York, NY
Painted Surfaces curated by Thomas Lollar, Albany Institute of History and Art, Albany, NY
"Materials as Media" curated by Virginia Roeder and Barbara Blades, Evanston Art Center, Evanston, IL

1985   Peter Plagens, Laurie Fendrick, Sue Johnson and Fred Burton, Jan Cicero Gallery, Chicago, IL
"70th Annual Indiana Artists Exhibition", Indianapolis Museum of Art, Indianapolis, IN

"Paint 1985" curated by Jerrold Maddox, Central Michigan University, Mt Pleasant, MI (traveling)

1984   Illinois Artists' Show, Artemisia, Chicago, IL
Invitational, Patrick King Contemporary Art, Indianapolis, IN

1983   Invitational, Contemporary Art Workshop, Chicago, IL
Faculty Exhibition, Herron School of Art, Herron Gallery, Indianapolis, IN

Residency Fellowships:

Virginia Center for the Creative Arts, Amherst, VA, 2003
Art Omi International Artists' Colony, Omi, NY, 2001
American Antiquarian Society, Worcester, MA, 2000
The Mac Dowell Colony, Peterborough, NH, 1999
Oberpfälzer Künstlerhaus, Schwandorf, Germany, 1999
Ragdale Foundation, Lake Forest, IL, 1999
Vermont Studio Center, Johnson, VT, 1999
Ox-Bow Program of The School of the Art Institute of Chicago, 1998
Women's Studio Workshop, Rosendale, NY, 1997
Virginia Center for the Creative Arts, Amherst, VA, 1995
The Mac Dowell Colony, Peterborough, NH, 1991
Virginia Center for the Creative Arts, Amherst, VA, 1990
The Mac Dowell Colony, Peterborough, NH, 1989
Millay Colony for the Arts, Austerlitz, NY, 1988
Hambidge Center for the Arts and Sciences, Rabun Gap, GA, 1987

Fellowships, Grants and Awards:

Pollock-Krasner Foundation Fellowship, 1998
Maryland State Arts Council, Individual Artist Award in Visual Arts: 2D, 1995
NEA Regional Fellowship in Painting /Mid Atlantic Arts Foundation, 1994
Faculty Development Grants, St. Mary's College of Maryland, 1994, 95, 96, 97, 98, 99, 00, 01, 02, 03, 04
Outstanding Faculty of the Year, Herron School of Art, I.U.P.U.I, 1985
New Jersey State Council on the Arts Fellowship, 1984
Augusta G. Hazard Fellowship in Painting, 1979
Hiram Gee Fellowship in Painting, 1979

Teaching :

St. Mary's College of Maryland, St. Mary's City, MD, 1993-present
Marymount Manhattan College, New York, NY, 1992-93
Parsons School of Design, New York, NY, 1987-89
Herron School of Art, Indiana University –Purdue University in Indianapolis, 1983-85

Publications (articles, artwork and essays by the artist):

ed. McKinley, James. New Letters: A Magazine of Writing and Art, University of Missouri at Kansas City, Vol. 67. No. 2, 2001, selected prints reproduced from The Alternate Encyclopedia, pages, 94, 116, 133, 139, and 143.

ed., Dunlap, Patricia. Mulberry Tree Papers, St. Mary's College of Maryland, Fall 1999, Vol. XXI, No. 1, "Science and Sensibilities" (photos).

The Chronicle of Higher Education, April 10, 1998, Vol. XLIV, No. 31, "An 'Artist-Naturalist Emerges From the World of Self-Referential Art," (photo)

ed. Karp, Diane. New Observations, Issue #116, Fall 1997, Artists on Art issue, "Sue Johnson, The Alternate Encyclopedia, pg. 35 (photo)

ed. McKinley, James. New Letters: A Magazine of Writing and Art, Vol. 62, No. 4, November-December 1996, University of Missouri at Kansas City, selected prints reproduced from The Alternate Encyclopedia.

ed. Hoffman, Jill. Mudfish No. 6, Art & Poetry, Box Turtle Press, New York, selected etchings from Evolutionary Paths reproduced, 1992.

ed. McKinley, James. New Letters: A Magazine of Writing and Art, Vol. 58, No. 1, University of Missouri at Kansas City, selected plates reproduced from, Premonition of a Natural History: Fireflies Burning, 1992.

Catalogues and curatorial essays:

Spooner, Peter. Sue Johnson: The Alternate Encyclopedia, 2004, Exhibition Catalogue, Tweed Museum of Art, University of Minnesota Duluth

McGregor, Jennifer. Glyndor Gallery, Wave Hill, Insecta Magnifica (brochure), May 2002, (photos).

Carr, Jeffrey. Boyden Gallery, St. Mary's College of Maryland, exhibition brochure, "The Nature of Nature," October 16 – November 23, 2002 (photos).

Byrn, Brian. The Midwest Museum of American Art (brochure), The Alternate Encyclopedia, July 2002 (photos).

Pomeroy, Jordana. "The Science of Nature and the Nature of Science," Fragments from The Alternate Encyclopedia, McLean Project for the Arts, January 2001 (photos).

Pollan, Andrea. "Hidden Worlds, Other Views," McLean Project for the Arts, Fragments from the Alternate Encyclopedia, January 2001 (photos).

Spooner, Peter. Botanica: Contemporary Art and the World of Plants, 1999, exhibition catalogue (photos).

Weintraub, Linda. Along the Garden Path, Delaware Center for the Contemporary Arts, July 1998 (photo).

Pollan, Andrea. The Washington Review, Vol. XXIV, No. 1, 1998, June/July, Special ArtSites 98 Edition, "Curio Cabinet of Hybrid Possibilities" catalogue essay to accompany the exhibition (photo)

Katzman, Laura. The Alternate Encyclopedia, Anderson Gallery, Virginia Commonwealth University, Richmond, Virginia (Oct. – Dec. 1996) and the Boyden Gallery, St. Mary's College of Maryland, St. Mary's City, Maryland (Jan-Feb 1997) (photos).

Ostrow, Saul. Mssr. B's Curio Shop, Thread Waxing Space, 1992 (photo).

Myers, Terry R. Triangle Artists' Workshop 1991 Exhibition, Bennington College, Usdan Gallery, Bennington, Vermont, 1992.

Paine, Morgan T. Animal Icons Too at Alverno College Art Gallery, Milwaukee, Wisconsin, 1985.

Exhibition Reviews:

Sargent, Sarah. Art Papers, exhibition review of NeoNaturalism, July-August 2002, (photo).

Coppens, Julie York. "Unnatural Selection: Artist Sue Johnson teases, fascinates viewers with Alternate Encyclopedia," South Bend Tribune, August 4, 2002, (photos).

Fulmer, Marcia. "Wonderfully strange world of Sue Johnson," The Truth (Elkhart, IN), July 25, 2002, (photo).

Zimmer, William. "With Webs and Wings: In an Insect Frame of Mind," The New York Times, May 12, 2002. Art review, Insecta Magnifica at Wave Hill's Glyndor Gallery.

O'Sullivan, Michael. "Johnson's Hybrids: A Breed Apart," The Washington Post, February 23, 2001 (photos).

Polanski, G. Jurek. Sue Johnson: Pages from The Alternate Encyclopedia, Artscope, November 14, 2000, exhibition review/online art journal.

"A Glimpse at the Garden, " The Muse: Plains Art Museum Newsletter, Fall 1999 (photo).

Grover, Jan Zita. Power amid roots and leaves: 'Botanica' artists see the beautiful, sinister and sexy side of plants," Duluth News Tribune, August 22, 1999.

Ungar, Nancy. The Rockville Gazette, June 17, 1998, "Salting the wounds of 20th century life." (ArtSites exhibition review)

Dorsey, John. The Baltimore Sun, Art Review, September 4, 1997.

Giuliano, Mike. The Baltimore City Paper, Art Review, September 10, 1997, (photo).

Horodner, Stuart. New Observations, Issue #114, Spring 1997, Frankenstein issue, "The F Word," (photo)

Johnston, John D. The Enterprise, "Put That in Your Funk and Wagnalls," January 22, 1997, exhibition review (photos).

ed. Rosenblatt, Jean. The Chronicle of Higher Education, "Domesticating the Wild," November 15, 1996 (photos).

Katzman, Laura. Art Papers, exhibition review of The Alternate Encyclopedia, Vol. 20, Issue 1, January-February 1996 (photo).

McCoy, Mary. The Washington Post, "Three at Drysdale," exhibition review, July 30, 1994.

Hirsch, Faye. The Print Collector's Newsletter, "The Press" at -Horodner-Romley Gallery, New York, Vol. XXV, No 2, May-June 1994.

Watkins, Ellen. The Star Ledger, "Museums offer spectacular exhibition focusing on the flower as eternal moment," exhibition review, Bergen Museum of Science and Art, July 4, 1993.

Cotter, Holland. The New York Times, exhibition review, "Nature Fabrilis" at Stiebel Modern, July 3, 1992.

Wilkin, Karen. Partisan Review, "At The Galleries," exhibition review of "Morphologic" at Art in General and "Beyond Nature" at Marymount Manhattan College Gallery, Vol. LIX No. 3, Summer 1992.

Wyatt, Julie. The Knickerbocker News, Albany, New York. "A fine, eclectic show at the Albany Institute of Art," 1985 (photo).

Taaffe, Susan. The New Art Examiner, exhibition review, "Anthropology Games" at the Columbus Cultural Art Center, Columbus, Ohio, 1985 (photo).

Garmel, Marion. The Indianapolis News, "Artist Sue Johnson measures civilization by the games we play," 1985 (photo).

Mannheimer, Steven. The Indianapolis Star, Indianapolis, IN "Work by Sue Johnson Featured in Two Exhibitions," 1985 (photo).

Public Collections:

    Bristol–Myers/Squibb
    The Prudential Life Insurance Company,
    Francis J. Greenburger Foundation
    Bucknell University Art Collection
    St. Mary's College of Maryland Art Collection
    Exxon Chemical Company
    Art Omi International Art Colony
    Tweed Museum of Art, University of Minnesota Duluth

Portrait of the artist, 2004
Photo: Colby Caldwell

UNIVERSITY ADMINISTRATION

University of Minnesota
Robert H. Bruininks, President
Board of Regents
David Metzen, Chair
Anthony R. Baraga, Vice Chair
Clyde Allen, Jr.
Peter Bell
Frank Berman
Dallas Bohnsack
John Frobenius
William Hogan
Richard McNamara
Lakeesha Ransom
Maureen K. Reed
Patricia Simmons

University of Minnesota Duluth
Kathryn A. Martin, Chancellor
Vincent R. Magnuson, Vice Chancellor for Academic Administration
Gregory R. Fox, Vice Chancellor for Finance and Operations
Bruce L. Gildseth, Vice Chancellor for Academic Support and Student Life
William Wade, Vice Chancellor for University Relations
Jack Bowman, Dean, School of Fine Arts
James Klueg, Interim Chair, Department of Art

TWEED MUSEUM OF ART ADVISORY BOARD
Kay Biga
Jack Bowman, Dean, School of Fine Arts
Florence Collins
Barb Gaddie
Adu Gindy
Beverly Goldfine
Bea Levey, Chair
Anne Lewis
Alice B. O'Connor
Henry Roberts
Robin Seiler
Dan Shogren
Ex-officio
Kathryn A. Martin, Chancellor
Vincent R. Magnuson, Vice Chancellor for Academic Administration
Peter F. Spooner, Interim Director, Tweed Museum of Art
Patti Tolo, Development Officer, School of Fine Arts

MUSEUM PERSONNEL

Tweed Museum of Art Staff
Will Bartsch, Work-Study (Technical)
Rose LaGrosse, Security
Susan Hudec, Museum Educator
Chong Johnson, Security
Steve Johnson, Security
Sandi Peterson, Senior Administrative Specialist
Kathy Sandstedt, Executive Administrative Specialist
Kim Schandel, Museum Store Manager
Delora Shaw, Work-Study (Clerical)
Peter F. Spooner, Interim Director / Curator
Peter Weizenegger, Preparator

Museum Interns, 2003-04
Selja Ojanne
Evan Williamson

Sue Johnson: The Alternate Encyclopedia

This project is funded in part by the Minnesota State Arts Board by an
appropriation from the Minnesota Legislature and the National Endowment
for the Arts; the Alice Tweed Tuohy Foundation;   and UMD Student Service Fees.

Catalogue design, Stephanie L. Magedanz

ISBN 1-889523-28-3

Tweed Museum of Art
University of Minnesota Duluth
1201 Ordean Court
Duluth, MN 55812
(218) 726-8222
fax (218) 726-8503
tma@d.umn.edu
www.tweedmuseum.org

*This activity is made
possible in part by a grant
from the Minnesota State
Arts Board, through an
appropriation by the
Minnesota State
Legislature and a
grant from the National
Endowment for the Arts.* MINNESOTA
STATE ARTS BOARD

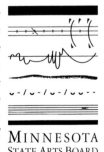